A Bird's-Eye View
of Life with ADD and ADHD:
Advice from Young Survivors!

"*A Bird's-Eye View of Life with ADD & ADHD: Advice from Young Survivors* will become a treasured resource for teenagers and their parents and teachers. What makes this book different from all others on the market (and there are many) is that one of the authors is a young adult with ADHD (Alex) and the other is his mother (Chris). They have collaborated to gather stories from a dozen other teenagers with ADHD. Together, they tell what life is like living with this condition and give practical advice on overcoming challenges. Alex's great sense of humor and his inspiring message of hope will make this book very worthwhile reading for teenagers who want the "behind-the-scenes" facts from two authors with a great deal of first-hand experience."
—**Harvey C. Parker, Ph.D.**, author of *Problem Solver Guide for Students with AD/HD*

"Everything in this book is sooooo me! I completely relate to the issues and the advice. This book is going to help many kids who are confused and uncertain about how to cope with their ADD."
—**Amelia Friedman**, age 19

"A wonderful book full of helpful facts and suggestions—written by teenagers with ADHD for teenagers with ADHD. This is the first time up-to-date information has been presented in this unique format—reporting teenagers' feelings and thoughts about living with this condition. Highly recommended reading for all teenagers experiencing the symptoms of ADHD!"
—**Theodore Mandelkorn, M.D.**, pediatrician, Director, Puget Sound Behavioral Medicine Center.

"I really love this book! It is an essential tool for any pre-teen or teen who is living with AD/HD."
—**Perry W. Green, III**, age 17

This authoritative guide for children and teens will be an indispensable tool for your home, school, or office!

In Memory of

Billie Tucker Dendy
1920-2003

A loving and devoted mother, grandmother,
and great grandmother
who always put others first!

A Bird's-Eye View
of Life with ADD and ADHD:
Advice from Young Survivors!

A Reference Book
for Children and Teenagers

By
Chris A. Zeigler Dendy
Alex Zeigler

Cherish the Children

The cover: "Lake jumping!"

In the cover picture, Alex is riding his bike off a ramp into a lake while his friend Chad looks on. This was a favorite pastime for him and a few of his friends when they were in high school. Of course not all his friends with ADD or ADHD were this daring. Ironically, the only person who ever got hurt doing this jump was an adult who didn't have ADHD—he was too cautious and tentative. <u>Note</u>: Obviously, this can be a dangerous activity and should be done only with parental supervision.

All rights reserved. Published in the United States of America by Cherish the Children. Questions should be addressed to the authors at one of these addresses:

Cherish the Children
P. O. Box 189
Cedar Bluff, Alabama 35959
chris@chrisdendy.com
Visit our web site: www.chrisdendy.com

Library of Congress Control Number: 2003094291

Zeigler Dendy, Chris A.
Zeigler, Alex
A Bird's–Eye View of Life with ADD and ADHD: Advice from Young Survivors / by Chris A. Zeigler Dendy and Alex Zeigler. — 1st ed.
p. cm.
Includes bibliographical references and index.
ISBN 0-9679911-3-7
1. Attention–deficit disorder—Popular works. 2. Attention–deficit disorder in children and adolescents.

First Edition

Dedication

This book is dedicated to
all the children and teenagers around the world
who valiantly struggle each day
to cope with the challenges of ADD and ADHD

and

our extraordinary teen experts
who were willing to tell their personal stories
to help others:

Adrian	Amelia
Ari	Erik
Jeremy	Kati
Katie	Khris
Kyle	Nathan
Perry	Tyler

About the Authors

Alex Zeigler, B.S.: Alex graduated from college with a major in Forensics and a minor in Computer Science. While in college he provided computer consultation and designed webpages, most notably www.chrisdendy.com. He was elected president of his criminal justice fraternity. He has given presentations about the challenges of living with an attention deficit at numerous conferences, including National CHADD. Currently he is working as a graphic artist and layout designer. In fact, he designed the cover and did the layout and graphic design for this book.

Chris Abney Zeigler Dendy, M.S.: Chris is an author with over 35 years experience as a former teacher, school psychologist, mental health counselor and administrator, national consultant on children's mental health and child advocate. She presents nationally and internationally on ADD and ADHD. Her books draw upon her extensive professional experience and more importantly upon her personal experience of parenting two now grown sons, one with ADD and the other ADHD. Her publications include:

Books: (Available at bookstores and public libraries everywhere.)
Teenagers with ADD and ADHD (over 73,000 copies sold)
Teaching Teenagers with ADD and ADHD

Videos: (Available from Cherish the Children.)
Teen to Teen: the ADD Experience (also available in Spanish)
Father to Father: the ADD Experience

Visit www.chrisdendy.com for more information.

Table of Contents

Caution from the Authors:

Please note that neither of the authors is a physician or medical researcher.

➤ Much of the information contained in this book reflects the personal experiences of the young people who were interviewed.

➤ Obviously medication should only be considered after a thorough evaluation by an appropriately trained and experienced physician. Medications affect each person differently and anyone considering medication should carefully investigate and monitor for side effects.

➤ The use of brand names of medications is not intended as an endorsement of specific products, but only to describe the actual experiences of the youth who were interviewed.

➤ The adult experts mentioned in the book, including Russell Barkley, Sam Goldstein, Tom Brown, Tim Wilens, Patricia Quinn, and Peter Jensen, are some of the country's leading researchers in the field of ADD and ADHD. Some, like Dr. Barkley, have devoted their entire professional careers researching ADHD. Others, like Ned Hallowell and Bob Brooks, offer inspirational insights about coping with this challenging condition. Patricia Quinn and Kathleen Nadeau have added new insights regarding the special challenges and needs of girls. Several helpful books are listed in the References & Resources section.

Acknowledgements

We have been fortunate to have extraordinary teens and adults work closely with us to ensure that this book is the very best we can make it. Careful research and input from many parents and professionals have helped make my previous books very successful. This time around we're pairing these wonderful parent and professional contributors with *exceptional teen experts.* Hopefully, as a result of our joint efforts, this book will be an indispensable tool for educating children and teenagers about coping successfully with ADD and ADHD. Several pediatricians, a psychiatrist, a school psychologist, an attorney, special education teachers, educational consultants, and most importantly, parents and teens reviewed the material and provided critical input. A special thank you goes to each of them.

William Buzogany, M.D.
Theodore Mandelkorn, M.D.
Gale Gordon, M.D.
Claudia Dickerson, Ph.D.
Nancy Shashaty, M.D.
Jeff Prince, M.D.
Mary Durheim, M.S.
Joan Helbing, M.S.
Jill Murphy, B.S.
Sharon Hodges, Ph.D.
Carol Robertson, B.S.
Lynn Groves, B.S.
Pamper Garner Crangle, B.S.
Matthew Cohen, J.D.

Several other people also made important contributions: Jay Durheim, Jon Gordon, Brianna Murphy, Janice Bond, Evelyn Green, Karran Royal, Misti Bass, Elizabeth Stephenson, Blanca Morales, Audrey Grabowski, and Bob, Beth, and Sara Butler.

Special Thanks to our Publishing Team

We're also deeply indebted to the superb professional skills of three key people who helped polish this diamond while it was still in the rough: Patricia Harmon, Jennifer Kinard, and Chris Carr. Patti was the primary editor for this book and did a truly superb job. Not only is she an extremely knowledgeable editor but she also has a strong commitment to educating people about attention deficit disorder. Thanks also to Chris Carr, an extraordinary artist and printing consultant, for his creative genius and guidance through the publishing process. We were also lucky that Patricia's sister, Jennifer, who is also an excellent editor, gave us a second set of eyes to review the material.

Publishing this book became a gratifying family affair. Alex assumed a dual role as coauthor and graphic artist. He designed the book cover, did the layout for the book, and coordinated with our printer. Dad and husband, Robert T. Dendy was one of our most important advisors.

Editor: Patricia L. Harman
Artist & printing consultant: Chris Carr
Layout graphic artist: Alex Zeigler

One Last Special Thank You

Thanks also to our parents and grandparents

Lillian Jennings Abney
1918-

Judge William L. Abney, Jr.
1916-1997

who gave us life, special talents,
and taught us compassion for others!

ADD & ADHD
according to Alex!

My name is Alex Zeigler and I was diagnosed with Attention Deficit Disorder when I was twelve years old. So if you're reading this book, then you probably have an attention deficit too.

Our family struggled with my attention deficit especially during my teenage years. Because we've been through some really tough times, my mother, Chris Zeigler Dendy, and I decided to write this book together to help you better understand yourself and your ADD or ADHD. We learned a lot of the lessons in this book the hard way, so we wanted to share those lessons in hopes that it will be a little easier for you and your family to cope with your attention deficit disorder.

At first I didn't know what it meant to have an attention deficit disorder. And if you're like me, you probably have lots of questions too. Hopefully this book will answer most of your questions.

There are several things that I wish I had known when I was first diagnosed. Looking back, one of the main things I wish somebody had told me is that

You aren't Stupid!
and
You aren't Lazy!

At times, when I was in high school I felt pretty stupid and thought that I must be lazy. Otherwise I would have done my schoolwork without my parents and teachers having to nag me so much. Struggling with my schoolwork was probably the worst part about having an attention deficit. I really wanted to do well in school and I tried really hard to pay attention. But I just couldn't do it. Although I did graduate from high school, I just barely got by in most of my classes.

I also wish someone had told me why I had trouble concentrating.

Later I learned that experts believe that our neurotransmitters—the chemical messengers of the brain—don't work exactly right when we need to pay attention. The three main neurotransmitters that control our ability to pay attention are *dopamine, norepinephrine,* and *serotonin.* These neurotransmitters carry the messages that help us pay attention.

Sometimes when a student with an attention deficit is trying to listen to his parents or teachers, it's like trying to send an electrical current along a wire where there are some bad connections. All the messages can't get through and your mind wanders, you may daydream, or you get distracted. If you want to read more about your brain and neurotransmitters, turn to the back of the book and read Appendix 5.

One of our primary goals for writing this book is to help you understand your attention deficit better. Here are a few suggestions about using this book:

➤ You may want to read the table of contents first to see which topics interest you.

➤ In the next section I'll introduce you to the teen experts who helped make this book possible. It may be fun to see which one is most like you.

➤ One section includes a list of thirteen unique challenges, such as forgetfulness and disorganization that many of us live with every day.

➤ When I was sixteen, I did an interview with my mother and talked about what my school years were like. If you're interested in knowing what school was like for me, you can read the interview in Appendix 1. Maybe some of the things I said then will help you now.

➤ If some of the terms confuse you or you don't know what they mean, we've also included an *ADD & ADHD Dictionary* at the end of the book in Appendix 10.

➤ In case your parents want to learn more, there will be additional information in the back that my mother wrote for them.

Let's not forget the positives. Although this book focuses on the challenges of living with an attention deficit, one thing we've got to do is to also recognize our strengths and special talents. Many of us have a wonderful zest for living and have high energy. Life is never dull when we're around. We often have creative ideas and unique ways of thinking about things. We can also hyperfocus and work on projects much longer than most people. In fact, sometimes, we become so engrossed in our projects that we lose all track of time.

You've got to find your special talents and develop them. For example, among the teen experts featured in this book there is a pretty good car mechanic, musician, and theater stage manager. Plus another hopes to be an attorney some day. Some of the others are too young to know what they want to do when they grow up but are developing skills now that will help them later.

So just be patient; one day you'll find your special skills and place in the world.

So with that introduction, let's get started.
Good Luck!!

P.S. Let me caution you before you read any further...

WARNING!

Do not try to read this book in one sitting!
It may be hazardous
to your health and family relationships!
The book length exceeds the attention limits
of teenagers with attention deficits.
Do not read for more than
twenty to thirty minutes at one time!

Meet the Real Experts
on ADD & ADHD

In this section, you'll hear from several teenagers and preteens ranging in age from 12 to 18 who also have ADD or ADHD. At times all of these teens have struggled with many of the same issues I faced. However, their challenges may be unique. For example, teens who are hyperactive will tell you about some of their special challenges. A few girls will also explain what coping with ADD or ADHD has been like for them. Even though we're all a little different, dealing with our ADD or ADHD has been a huge struggle for all of us.

All of these teens have given great tips for how they're coping with their attention deficit. And as you might expect, the older teens have more experience and consequently, give more tips. But, we have to be honest and say up front that even *we* don't follow our own advice all the time. We have good intentions, but it's just plain hard to always remember to follow through on them.

Almost all of these teens have found that medication has helped them cope better with their attention deficit. In fact they may tell you which medicine they're currently taking. The teens are not all taking the same medication; there were several different ones that are effective. Unfortunately, one teen has not been able to find a medicine that works best for him. Just remember that a medication that works for one of our teen experts, may not work for you. The key is to talk with your doctor to find the treatment that's best for you. Of course you already know that medicine is not going to magically "cure" you; you'll still have to work very hard and learn new skills to cope with your attention deficit.

Most of these teens share at least eight to ten of the thirteen challenges I experienced with my ADD inattentive. Some share all thirteen regardless of whether they have ADD or ADHD.

One of the impressive things about all these teenagers is that they have such exciting and unique interests. Frequently, their special gifts and talents fall outside of the classroom. With all of the negative experiences that occur at school, these talents are what make these teens feel special. Each of us must find the skills we're good at and strengthen and develop these special talents and gifts! I hope you'll enjoy reading about the special talents of these teenagers and get some ideas for developing your own unique talents.

ADHD according to Nathan (12)

Nathan is an active middle school student who participates in many sports, including street hockey, skateboarding, baseball, and basketball. His two favorite pastimes are playing street hockey and playing with his Game Boy Advance. This year he attended a summer camp that included training in street hockey. Every day he practiced handling the puck, shooting, skating, passing and being a good team player. Last year, his team scored 20 points, and Nathan scored 4 goals and had three assists. He quickly learned that street hockey is a team sport because there is no "I" in team. One year, Nathan's team, won the league championship. Luckily, the boys received some coaching tips from members of the Memphis-based River Kings semi-pro ice hockey team. And according to a press release by the River Kings, Nathan was the star of the game with three goals and three assists.

Nathan has a wide variety of interests ranging from reading to music to stamp collecting. Reading is something he really enjoys, especially the Harry Potter and the Chicken Soup series. Music is another one of his passions. Recently, he began playing with the hand bells group at church. He also plays the snare drum in his middle school band.

Nathan works really hard at school and makes mostly A's and B's. Medication has worked well for him (Strattera) so he has not needed any accommodations or special supports like untimed tests. On the other hand, he has problems with many of the same things his Uncle Alex does. For example, he has to work closely with his parents to stay organized. His best class is social studies and his worst one is math. Because of his messy handwriting and difficulty lining up numbers, he is more likely to make mistakes and sometimes struggles in math.

ADHD according to Katie (13)

Katie is an eighth grade middle school student who loves hanging out with and talking to her friends. She also enjoys several sports activities such as snow skiing, volleyball, horseback riding, and biking. She loves to ski downhill and also wants to learn to snowboard. One year she received an award for the most improved player on her volleyball team. She was also selected as a cheerleader for both football and basketball. In her community, she volunteers as a mentor for a child with Down syndrome. In addition, her high school requires students to do community service for graduation, so she plans to volunteer at a nursing home. As a trained certified babysitter, she is very popular and in great demand to sit with children in the neighborhood. Last year, she was invited to speak about her attention deficit at the national CHADD Conference. CHADD is a national organization that provides educational information about Children and Adults with Attention-Deficit/Hyperactivity Disorders.

Taking Adderall XR has really improved her ability to pay attention at school. She works extremely hard, does her schoolwork without being asked to do so, and is making mostly A's and B's. History is her favorite subject and math is probably her worst class. Although written expression is hard for her, she has learned new skills to compensate for this problem.

Even though she has ADHD, she struggles with many of the same challenges that Alex does. The toughest thing at school is when she has to memorize information like math facts or formulas. Luckily, she doesn't have any problems with organization, forgetfulness, or procrastination.

ADHD according to Kyle (13)

Speaking of great adventures, would you believe that one year Kyle's Boy Scout Troop 36 went on a 108-mile canoe trip on the Missouri River? Being a member of Kyle's scout troop is really fun. Every year they go on a "fifty-miler" which may include a 108 mile canoe trip, a hike around Mt. Rainier, or a seven day beach hike.

When Kyle wants to relax after school, he loves to climb on his Honda 200 FatCat dirt bike and ride up and down hills on his family's property. He needs alone time to unwind after a rough day at school and riding his dirt bike is the perfect escape. Even the rain doesn't stop him from riding his bike. After all, riding through huge mud puddles and getting covered with mud can be a lot of fun. Snowboarding and wrestling are also sports that have recently captured his interest. He also loves to sing and is a member of the high school jazz choir.

Kyle is quite skilled with his computer. He loves to take it apart and put it back together. Once he hooked up two of his computers to the phone line and recorded an interview with a friend who was in flight training school. He also figured out how to do voice-overs for recordings on the computer. If anyone has computer problems at home, they come to Kyle to figure out the glitch and repair it.

Language arts is probably his best subject and his worst class is science. Of course, medication (Concerta) really helps him concentrate at school. Last year, he had to keep a lab book organized and that was a nightmare. He can't read his own handwriting. He also doesn't do well in classes with a fast talking teacher. It takes him a long time to process information and he needs someone to repeat things for him. Sometimes he will be thinking so hard that he doesn't even realize that he actually spoke aloud—a habit that has gotten him into trouble with some of his teachers.

The hardest thing about ADHD for Kyle is having good social relationships. Sometimes people say that he is a loner, but at other times he is a very social teen who enjoys talking with people of all ages. He is especially bothered by gossip, mainly when he knows it's not true. Rather than letting it pass, he confronts whoever is gossiping. It makes him very angry when someone else gets hurt. He sees himself as an advocate for those people and will fight on their behalf if necessary; otherwise, he avoids fighting.

ADHD according to Kati (14)

Art, music, and acting have been the center of Kati's world for her whole life. During the summers she often attends art camps in Tennessee. Her family loves her pictures and has hung several in the house. Her mother is especially proud of the furniture Kati painted to match the kitchen. She drew beautiful flowers and leaves on a kitchen stool. She also loves pottery and photography. She currently enjoys fencing and was invited to participate in the National Fencing Competition.

Musically, Kati expresses her talents by playing the viola. This instrument is similar to a violin, but is larger and has a more mellow sound. As a member of her middle school orchestra, she plays harmony on the viola. She recently started playing the drums and hopes to get a set for Christmas.

She loves to act and has been in all the plays her middle school has produced. This year she had the lead role in a murder mystery play. She loved the challenge of being the murderer! This was one of those wonderful situations where you get to scream, yell and be evil and people still love you.

Unlike most students with ADHD, Kati loves reading and writing essays. She wrote a poem during the seventh grade that was submitted to a national competition. It was one of ten selected for publication in a book, *A Celebration of Young Poets*. But math is another story; it's her worst subject.

Kati's school is very demanding, especially since she attends a private college prep school. Of course, private schools run by religious groups are not mandated by law to have special educational plans known as IEPs or Section 504 Plans for students so Kati doesn't get much in the way of accommodations. However, the school does give her extended time on tests.

Taking tests is not easy for Kati. Sometimes the way the teacher asks the questions on multiple choice tests make them especially hard for her. For example, "Which of the following is *not* true?" Or at times when there are two-part questions, she may forget to answer the second part of a question. If she doesn't know an answer to a test question, but thinks she should, her anxiety increases. It's like she gets stuck on that question and can't really think clearly about the rest of the test. Long tests are also overwhelming to her. If there is a page full of problems, she worries that she can't finish them. Then she begins to wonder, what's the use of even trying?

ADHD according to Tyler (15)

Tyler's passion in life is playing soccer. He began playing soccer when he was six and has played on recreation teams for the past nine years. This year, he plays left defensive end on his high school soccer team. In middle school, Tyler was one of the fastest players on his team. His teammates nicknamed him *Spiderman*, because he would steal the ball away from the other team so quickly that they hardly knew what had happened. In middle school, he was the goalie and the other teams rarely scored against him. His friends joked that it was like he had glue on his gloves. He took up golf at age eleven, which he enjoys playing with his dad. Tyler and his father also share a love of boating and fishing.

Tyler and his closest friend, who has ADD, love to escape from the pressures of school by playing paintball together. They will meet ten or so friends, divide into teams, and have great paintball battles in the woods behind their homes. Everyone comes dressed from head to toe in camouflage clothes and sometimes with paint on their faces. The paintball gun contains a CO_2 cartridge that makes the ball shoot out pretty hard. Because getting shot is painful, nearly everyone wears masks, vests, gloves, hats, and other protective gear.

Tyler also loves singing bass in his seventy-five member high school men's choir. He works very hard and is an invaluable asset to the choir. One year he received the Humanitarian Award for his willingness to help above and beyond the call of duty.

School is really hard for Tyler. He has to study twice as much as other students. Since English is his worst subject, he has a tutor who is helping him improve his writing skills. He has gotten pretty good at writing a basic five-paragraph essay. He is also lucky that he is a good test taker. Math is probably his best subject. Like Alex, he has problems with most of the issues listed in this book, especially procrastination and forgetfulness. For Tyler, the toughest thing about having ADHD is just remembering to take his second dose of medication.

ADD according to Ari (15)

Ari can think of a lot of things he would rather be doing than schoolwork. Although he is modest about his accomplishments, he is really good at several sports: skateboarding, wakeboarding, surfing, snowboarding, scuba diving, and swimming. He has gone all over the country to attend special summer camps for his wakeboarding, skateboarding, and scuba diving. He has done underwater photography and hopes to learn to shoot underwater videos. He can do several tricks on his skateboard. He can do "foot kicks" and a "360." He has also mastered a somersault in the air known as a "tantrum" on his wakeboard.

Because of the warm weather in California, typically he swims at least four times a week almost year round. He gets lots of practice doing his swan dives and back dives, plus he works out almost everyday at the gym. Most of his friends have ADD or ADHD too, and he really likes hanging out with them. They like to surf, skateboard, play video games, eat a lot, and ride their go-peds, which are motorized scooters. Ari is very popular with his classmates; they honored him by electing him to the homecoming court one year.

Ari explains that he can identify with several challenges that Alex mentions. For example, before he started taking medicine, his biggest problem was trying to pay attention. Now that he is taking Adderall he can pay attention much better. Memorizing math facts was always really hard for him too. He is eligible for some accommodations if he wants them, for example, use of a multiplication chart, calculator, or math clues. Biology is his best subject and math is his worst. Like Alex, he prefers to print and he describes his handwriting as messy. It usually takes him longer to do his homework and finish tests than his classmates. Most of all he really hates working on big school projects. Ari figures, "Why not wait and do it the night before? At least then you're not miserable all week!"

ADHD according to Adrian (16)

One of Adrian's special talents is that he is bilingual. He speaks both English and Spanish. Adrian was born in Puerto Rico and moved to Georgia about four years ago. At first it was really tough because he didn't speak much English. But he learned quickly and now speaks both languages fluently.

Adrian has impressive mechanical skills. He loves working on his low rider bike. He takes a lot of pride in the fact that he has customized his low rider. The bike came in pieces and he had to put it all together piece by piece. The bike has several special features. He lowered the frame so that it's only three inches off the ground. His bike has wire rims, a brand new sparkling black banana seat, and a unique twisted kickstand. Everything else he added to the candy green frame is chrome. He has added mirrors, rims with 68 spokes and white wall tires. He plans to enter his bike in a low rider show in the fall. They give special prizes including money or trophies to the winners.

For fun, he likes to play pool with his dad two or three times a week. Of course school is not much fun at all. To express how he feels about his life, he likes to draw. His drawings may look like graffiti but he doesn't tag it, in other words he doesn't put it on walls. For example he once drew a spider web to show that at times he feels trapped. Once he drew faces showing that you may smile now but cry later. Some people misunderstand and think drawing graffiti is gang related but that's not true.

Adrian has found that school is extremely stressful. Although he is really good in math, like Alex, he would prefer to just write the answer only. He likes to take short cuts in his head and doesn't always show the steps in a problem. Memorization is really tough for him. That means physics is extra hard because the teacher wants him to memorize all the formulas. Tests are also difficult for him; it helps to be tested in a quiet room away from his class. Writing essays is also challenging. The good news is that he has a school case manger who arranges for him to get the help he needs to be successful.

ADHD according to Khris (16)

For Khris, music is his life! Since he was a little kid he has known that he wanted to be a jazz musician when he grew up. And now he is! His musical training started when he was seven years old. By middle school, he was playing in the marching band and now he plays in his high school jazz band. He has also started his own band, the Khris Royal Quartet. His group plays at weddings and other events in New Orleans. Most recently he had to decline a request to play at Tulane's graduation so that he could accept an invitation to play in Cuba for Chucho Valdez, an Afro-Cuban jazz pianist. In addition to performing, he also writes music and has done some recording.

Khris has been performing at the New Orleans Jazz and Heritage Festival since he was 8 years old. After attending Boston's Berklee College of Music this summer, he was awarded a scholarship for study after his high school graduation. He plans to pursue a career in music.

Khris attends a regular high school each morning and in the afternoon from 1:00 to 5:00 he attends the New Orleans Center for Creative Arts (NOCCA). This is the same school that jazz great Wynton Marsalis attended. In fact, Khris has had the honor of playing for Marsalis and even played basketball with him.

School, however, is a different story. His morning classes are his least favorite time of day. Music is constantly popping into his head all day and he has to ignore it so he can pay attention in class. Although he struggles with many of the same challenges that Alex and the others face, the good news is that he is passing all of his classes. Forgetfulness, especially with homework assignments, has been a big problem for him. Through his IEP (Individualized Education Program), he is eligible for shortened assignments and extra time for assignments and tests. Luckily, he also has a resource teacher who is really helpful with organizational skills. The school also provides him with a laptop computer.

ADD according to Perry (17)

If you think you may need a good persuasive attorney one day, then keep Perry in mind. As a senior, he is captain of his high school debate team. A four-year member of the team, he is also a founding member. Obviously, Perry is an experienced debater and is rated as one of the top twenty debaters in Chicago. He loves the debate tournaments that are scheduled on Friday and Saturday once a month. Although the debates are competitive, they're also a lot of fun. Over the years, he has made many friends.

Currently, he is interning with a local law firm and is well on his way to becoming an attorney one day. He works fifteen hours a week, which typically means three or so hours every day. The money from his internship enabled him to buy a Palm Pilot.

Perry says it took him seventeen years to figure out what school was all about and how to play the game to be successful. He credits his Palm Pilot for helping him be more organized and successful in school. He loves his advanced placement government, politics and history classes. Currently, he is earning college credits through a joint program with DePaul University. He is proud of the "B" he has earned in his college-level political science class.

As for challenges at school, Perry, like so many students with ADD inattentive, often forgets his homework. Memorizing math facts was really hard for him too. Trying to remember math formulas for tests was often a nightmare and made him feel anxious in class. Foreign languages and time management are also very challenging for him.

When he was in ninth grade he rebelled against taking medication for a while. Then he realized he had a problem and needed to do something to help himself plan and get organized for his debates. Adderall has really helped him with his research and competition in debates. Like most teens with an attention deficit, impulsive spending is also a big issue for him. That problem, however, has changed somewhat since he has gotten a job and is spending his own money. As a result, he has found that he takes better care of his possessions and is more careful with his money.

ADHD according to Jeremy (17)

Around Jeremy's house he is known as "Mr. Fix-it." He is really a hands-on kind of guy. He can repair or operate just about anything mechanical from a car to the VCR and computer. Over the last several years he has taught himself to do computer programming. Anytime anything goes wrong with the family computer, his parents call on him to get it operating again. He loves working on cars and likes to make modifications that make them go faster. Right now he is modifying his own car into a drag racer. In addition, he installed a sound system in his car. His other interests include playing the guitar and drawing. A few years ago, he won first place in an art show.

Jeremy attends a private school and loves going to football games. He is so enthusiastic about the team that he was awarded the "Spirit Stick" for best school spirit.

Through the school's internship program, Jeremy is getting some great job experience at a heating and air conditioning business. Luckily, they have racing cars too and Jeremy gets to go to the race track with them. Sometimes during practice he works as part of the pit crew, changing the tires, fueling up the car, or just washing it. He loves just being at the track.

Volunteering is also something that's very important to Jeremy. He is a very thoughtful and compassionate person and helping other people is second nature to him. He has volunteered at a homeless shelter and served as a counselor for some of the children's activities in his church.

For Jeremy, one of the toughest challenges is to actually realize that he has ADHD and that he must struggle with it every single day. Some days he wants to deny he has it. School is challenging for Jeremy but unlike most students with attention deficits, math is his best subject. He finds English boring so it's not one of his favorites. Writing is so frustrating for him especially remembering the rules for spelling and grammar. Like many students with an attention deficit, forgetting assignments and procrastination are big problems for Jeremy. He also struggles with getting up and making it to school on time. Jeremy plans to take the ACT untimed this year so that he can attend a local community college.

ADHD according to Erik (18)

Like many teenagers with ADHD, Erik is very active, loves being around people, and enjoys a wide variety of activities. Recreational sports are fun for him, especially pick-up games of basketball. He also loves Ultimate Frisbee which is like an on-going football game that never stops. Socializing with friends at his high school football games, church youth group events, and church camp are very important to him. Video games are another passion for him, especially "Halo" on Microsoft's XBox system. Like many other teenage boys, eating and sleeping are top priorities too.

As for school, writing essays is probably the hardest thing for him. He has great ideas, but finds it hard to organize and get them in the right order. Luckily he has a great memory and is good with words. That helps him write good essays. In addition, taking Concerta has really helped Erik do better in school. Science and math are his toughest subjects. Like many students with attention deficits, he reports that he does better in classes if he likes the teacher. The opposite is also true; he does poorly in classes where he doesn't like the teacher. In spite of these challenges, Erik's college prep English is still his best class. He also likes history and wrote a special report on the Individuals with Disabilities Education Act (IDEA), the federal education law. The paper was so good that it earned him an A. Research on this project really had a profound impact on his life.

When he was in middle school, classes were so horrible for him that he became very discouraged. He struggled with most of the same things Alex did. Paying attention, organizational skills, taking notes, and completing all of his work were especially difficult for him. However, having a good IEP, which is mandated by IDEA, made all the difference for him. He has developed new skills that help him cope effectively with his ADHD. When he graduates, he is planning to attend a community college in Washington State.

ADD according to Amelia (18)

Amelia has been making clothes for dolls and bears since she was six years old. So it comes as no surprise that she is pursing a career in theater, with an emphasis on stage management and prop and costume creation. She is currently a freshman at the University of the Ozarks, which offers a unique theater program. Previously, she attended a special high school for students who were especially good in the arts and theater. Acting, however, is not her thing; instead, she loves being the "techie," the person behind the scenes who makes the play run well. Her passions include stage management, managing the sound system, building props and making costumes. One of her most difficult prop challenges came her senior year when she built a candlestick telephone circa 1905. Her creation was made of PVC pipe, drip pans from a stove, Styrofoam, plenty of tape and lots of black paint. It looked great on stage. She also made six costumes for the production of "My Fair Lady" that included six corsets. Many of the costumes had to be sewn by hand.

She also loves to swim and work on jigsaw puzzles. She can work on puzzles for hours; often finishing up the 1000-piece puzzles in four days or less. In high school, when she couldn't sleep at night, which was pretty often, she would sneak out and work on puzzles until she felt sleepy. Sometimes she would talk on the phone with her friends and work on a puzzle at the same time. Clearly, multi-tasking is not a problem for her.

Every single challenge that Alex talks about presents problems for Amelia too. Disorganization, forgetfulness, sleep problems, and math are all huge challenges for her. She has to work so hard at being organized. Occasionally, she forgets to take her medication until halfway through her college English class. Fortunately, the professor is so interesting that he keeps her attention. So she simply takes her medicine (Adderall XR) when she finally remembers it. Memorizing has also been tough for her.

Her lack of sleep is a major challenge right now. Sleep deprivation presents problems because she dozes off in class and feels grumpy which puts a strain on her friendships. She describes herself as a night person and explains that she does much of her best writing late at night.

Although she didn't have an IEP or accommodations when she was in high school, she had to work extra hard to make her A's and B's. Her homework often took at least four or five hours to finish each day.

Authors' notes:

➤ Two additional young people, Aaron and Ashley, provided advice for our book after our twelve teen experts had been selected.

➤ If, after reading our book, you have some favorite strategies that work for you, send them to us by e-mail at chris@chrisdendy.com. Thanks! We can use them to help other teens.

Chapter 2

Overcoming Common Challenges of ADD & ADHD

Most of us learned the basics about ADD and ADHD from our parents, doctor or counselor. Some aspects of an attention deficit are obvious: we have trouble paying attention and we're forgetful. But beyond the basics, you may also be wondering what made your doctor say that you have an attention deficit. If you're curious, you may want to read Appendix 2 before reading the rest of this section. This appendix explains the characteristics doctors look for when they diagnose ADD or ADHD.

You also need to know about all the challenges that sometimes come along with having an attention deficit—challenges you may never have heard about before. Some of the things we do that drive our parents and teachers crazy are related to our ADD or ADHD, but not everyone realizes this. For example, lots of us have trouble getting organized for school and remembering our homework assignments. At times, we lose things like our books, clothes or even our completed homework. Some of us have trouble falling asleep or waking up, so we have morning fights with our parents about getting to school on time. Others may have trouble measuring the passage of time and frequently are late. It's my hope that the insights we offer in this book will help you to understand yourself and your attention deficit better.

In this section I'll be talking about how ADD inattentive affected me. Of course, the same may not be true for you. For example, if you have ADHD, some things may not apply to you. Experts tell us that people with an attention deficit are not all alike: each person is unique. Some teenagers also struggle with other challenges, known as *coexisting conditions*. These may include learning disabilities, anxiety, and depression. This means that for some of us, our attention deficit is more serious, whereas for others, it's very mild. Hopefully, you'll be lucky and not have to deal with all the challenges we have listed on the next page.

Here is a list of unique challenges that often come with having ADD and ADHD. Which ones sound like you?

> Disorganized
> Inattentive
> Forgetful
> Impulsive
> Late—can't accurately judge the passage of time
> Problems falling asleep and waking up
> Messy handwriting
> Slow reading and writing or rushing through schoolwork
> Problems writing essays and reports
> Difficulty memorizing math facts and formulas
> Procrastinate
> Difficulty controlling emotions
> Restless: hyperactive

In this book, my mom and I have given you some ideas for ways to cope with these problems. In addition, the teens you read about earlier will give you some tips on strategies they have found helpful. However, these are just suggestions for you to consider. You've probably already developed some very good strategies for handling these challenges. But if you're still struggling with some of these issues, our teen experts may help you come up with some new ideas for tackling these problems. The important thing is for *you* to select a strategy that will work best for you. Now let's get started by talking about disorganization.

Chaos & Clutter

(disorganization)

You know you have an attention deficit if…[1]

⇒ Your parents refer to your messy backpack as the "black hole"; schoolwork goes in but is never seen again.

⇒ You did your homework but you don't have a clue where it is.

⇒ Your parents say your room looks like someone dropped an atomic bomb in it.

⇒ Cleaning up your room means shoving everything under the bed or in the closet.

⇒ Your carpet is covered with so much junk that you can't remember what color it is.

⇒ You take things apart but never put them back together again.

Fact: Most students with attention deficits are very disorganized. In fact, most of us have messy rooms, backpacks, lockers, and for some older teens, messy cars. But of course, that's not true for everyone (my brother kept his car spotless).

Teens with ADD and ADHD are often thought of as "visual organizers"—that means we like to be able to see where things are. Sometimes we hate to put games and tools away out of sight because we can't always remember where we put them.

I know I'm a visual organizer. Although I may look totally disorganized, I'm actually pretty organized in my own way. Most of the time I can find things within three minutes which time management experts say indicates a pretty good level of organization. I usually know where my tools are, because I can see them in my mind. It's like I have a mental map of where I used them last.

---

[1] The humorous but true stories included in this chapter have occurred to a variety of students with ADD or ADHD who shall remain nameless to protect the guilty.

To be organized you must have some special skills that include:

❶ having a good memory,

❷ figuring out the problem,

❸ developing a logical plan to solve the problem

❹ making yourself get started on the plan.

These important skills are sometimes called *executive functions.* Unfortunately, many of us with ADD or ADHD lack some of these critical executive function skills. If you're interested, there is more information about executive function in Appendix 8. Although there are medicines to help you pay attention, there are no medicines to specifically help with executive function problems such as disorganization and difficulty planning ahead. Hopefully scientists will find some new medicines to improve executive function skills so that you can be better organized and plan for the future more easily.

Unfortunately, some adults think that teens with attention deficits are less mature and responsible than their friends who don't have attention deficits. In fact, experts tell us that students with ADD and ADHD mature four to six years later than their friends. So, in many ways, a 16-year-old with an attention deficit is going to act more like he or she is 10 or 11. Of course, none of us likes hearing this news. Having this *developmental delay,* however, means that many of us will need *more* supervision and support at a time when most parents and teachers believe they should be giving us less supervision. And most likely you also think adults should be less involved in your life! In truth, each of us wants to be our own boss NOW.

As far as seeking independence from parents goes, many teens with attention deficits feel that they should have the freedom of a 21-year-old. That means we're always pushing for more freedom, while our parents are trying to slow that process down. Sometimes my parents referred to that as "pushing the envelope."

Getting Organized at Home

I know disorganization is a huge problem for me and is something I need to work on. Everyone wants to be able to find things; I know I do. When my room is really messy, clothes and games get lost. Then I have to waste time looking for them. When I'm already running late, I don't have time to hunt for something lost in the rubble. And sometimes I do feel embarrassed when friends come over and my room looks like a pigsty. When I was in high school, our garage was such a disaster; we couldn't even park a car in it.

> **My room.** My room was always messy. At first my parents fussed a lot, but they finally gave up and just shut the door.

> **Taking things apart.** I was always curious and loved to take gadgets apart. Then I would leave the pieces lying all over the carpet. My parents said we had an "electronic graveyard" at our house from all the things I took apart but never put back together.

> **Why I'm messy.** Ideas are always popping into my mind. So before I can finish and clean up after one project, I get another idea that leads to another project. I always think of something else that has to be done right away. Other times, I get too focused on one thing and before I know it, I haven't done anything else I was supposed to do that day. So, I hurry on to the next project and leave my mess in the middle of the floor.

By the end of the day, I'm burned out. The next morning, when I get up, I forget to clean up my first project. Later when I look at the mess, I feel totally overwhelmed with it and have no idea where to begin or what to do first. Sometimes when I'm cleaning, I don't know where to put things. I figure it will take forever anyway, so why bother.

Advice on Getting Organized at Home

Alex's Advice:

Here are some ideas that help me get organized—most of the time.

Getting your room organized.

> **Set aside time to clean up your room.** I usually knew it was time to clean my room when my mother couldn't walk across the floor to my bed without falling over something. Work out a cleaning schedule with your parents. Pick a time when you're

not rushed and can have a couple of uninterrupted hours to work on it.

➤ **Consider taking medication.** It's easier for me to clean my room and stay focused when my medicine is working.

➤ **Divide your room into sections.** If you need to "see" the sections of your room, take some rope or yellow "crime scene" tape and divide it into four to six sections. Start working in one section until it is clean. Continue cleaning until it is all done.

➤ **Organize everything to be cleaned up into three or four categories.** Organize them in two or three laundry baskets plus a garbage can. One basket may be for things to take to the kitchen, another for dirty laundry, and the third may be for clothes to be hung up. Of course throw away all your garbage.

➤ **Stay focused.** Make yourself stay focused. Don't let yourself get distracted when you're going through things. Sometimes I'll find something that I've been looking for for months. I always want to stop and work on whatever treasure I've just found. I totally forget that I'm supposed to be cleaning my room.

➤ **Set aside some things for later.** One way to avoid getting distracted is to start a "come back to later pile" that you can work on after you finish cleaning your room.

➤ **Set a timer to go off every 15 minutes as a reminder.** Ask yourself, "Am I doing what I'm supposed to be doing?"

➤ **Get your parents to help.** Ask your parents to clean the room with you. That way, after you understand what they mean when they say "clean up," you can do it on your own.

  ➤ Make a list of what your parents mean when they say "clean up your room." For example, make the bed, put your dirty clothes in the hamper, put your games away, hang up your clothes, and vacuum.

Amelia's Advice:

➤ **Listen to music.** When I clean my room, I listen to music. It keeps me interested and keeps me from getting distracted.

Nathan's Advice:

➤ **Organize your room.** It's really important to learn how to keep your room organized. I feel better when my room is cleaned up. My mother and I installed some shelves in my closet so I could organize my games and clothes. We have lots of shelves, plus clear containers so you can see everything easily. We also labeled each section to help me remember where to put things away. It's always easier to remember where things are when you can see them in your mind.

Getting Organized at School

My desk, backpack and locker were always messy. They were stuffed with loose papers, books, notebooks, clothes and who knows what else. My parents called my desk the "black hole" because schoolwork would go into it and disappear forever. A lot of times I did my homework, but would lose it or just forget to turn it in.

Once I had a teacher in an advanced biology class who wanted us to keep a detailed running log of all our assignments, dates assigned, our grades, and grade averages. With my organizational problems and weak executive function skills, there was no way I could do that. At that time I didn't know that disorganization was a characteristic of my attention deficit and that I could get accommodations. Instead, I transferred into a regular biology class.

Advice on Getting Organized at School

Alex's Advice:

➤ **Ask for accommodations, if needed.** If you have an attention deficit that interferes with your ability to learn, most schools will provide extra help known as accommodations. Disorganization and forgetfulness are such major problems for us, you may want to ask for accommodations or special support to help you be more organized and remember important things like homework assignments.

➤ **Organize your school locker or backpack.** Develop a system that works for you. For example, if you frequently forget to take your books home after school, try one of the following tips.

➢ **Put homework books together.** Each time you go back to your locker, put all of your books together that you need to take home that day. Find a way to mark them, maybe with Post-it notes.

➢ **Set aside one area in the locker.** Make a special section in the locker for your homework books. Use a shelf or divide the locker with a florescent clipboard or colorful poster board. Put the books you need to take home on the right side of the board.

➢ **Ask for help.** Maybe a teacher or a friend can help you organize your locker.

➢ **Keep schoolwork organized.** Although I hate to admit it, I needed help keeping my school papers organized. So once a week, my parents and I went through and cleaned out my notebook. You may ask your parents to help you do the same thing. We pulled out all of the old assignments and saved them until after the semester was over—just in case any of my homework assignments had not been turned into the teacher.

➢ **Ask for help with a "class log".** Keeping a log is incredibly difficult for us. Someone has to teach us how to keep a daily log of assignments and grades plus help us keep it up to date. Maybe you can work with a friend in class each day who can help you update your log. If a log is required, assistance could be included as an accommodation in your *IEP* or *Section 504 Plan*.

➢ **Use an electronic device.** If you're really forgetful, you might buy something fairly inexpensive like a Sharp *Wizard* or a *Zire* that you can type your assignments into and list meetings or due dates for big projects. Since it's always more fun to use an electronic gadget, you may be more likely to remember to write down your assignments. Older students may be ready for a more expensive *Palm Pilot* or pocket PC. They are fantastic! That's what really keeps me organized now. The pocket PC can help you keep up with many different projects, and it will beep to remind you when something is due or when it's time to take your medication.

➢ **Use a small notebook.** You can also make lists in a small 3" x 4" spiral notebook. You don't need to have an electronic device to write notes to yourself.

Nathan's Advice:

➤ **Use notebook dividers.** I have a two-inch notebook with dividers and pockets for every subject. That way I can put my handouts or homework in the pockets and don't lose them.

Amelia's Advice:

➤ **Use different folders for each class.** For school, I use separate folders for each class and make myself put papers in the back flap with my assignments in consecutive order. To keep from losing papers, I make several copies because I know I'm going to lose the first one.

Jeremy's Advice:

➤ **Buy a day planner.** My mother bought me a day planner and that has helped me be better organized. I keep everything in my day planner including all of my assignments and projects. So if I can't find my planner, I'm really lost. If I find myself worrying that I've forgotten something, I'll double-check my planner just to be safe.

Khris's Advice:

➤ **Use a Palm Pilot.** Trying to stay organized is one of my biggest problems. My Palm Pilot has been a huge help for me. I always put my schedule into it, my homework assignments, where I need to be, and what I need for the activity.

Daydreamers & Space Cadets

You know you have an attention deficit if...

⇒ You don't hear a word your mother says when she's talking. All you can see is her mouth moving.

⇒ You read a whole page and suddenly realize you can't remember a thing you've read. You have to start all over and read it again.

⇒ Your math teacher begins by saying, "Today we're going to talk about..." Then the next thing you hear is, "Mr. Zeigler, what are your thoughts about that?"

⇒ You're watching TV and suddenly your dad yells at you! Although he has been talking for five minutes, the first words that you actually hear are, "!#&%*. Don't you ignore me."

⇒ "Earth to Jeffrey" is your nickname from preschool.

⇒ Once when you forgot to take your medicine, you actually ran a red light and later stopped at a green light.

⇒ You were concentrating on driving the car and had no clue that you were speeding until the blue lights went on behind you.

Fact: Inattention or difficulty paying attention is one of the main characteristics of attention deficit disorders. But it comes as no surprise to us, our parents and our teachers that even though we have an attention deficit we can, in fact, pay attention...under certain circumstances. You probably know—from experience—that you can actually hyperfocus to the point where you lose all track of time and may spend hours on the computer or playing with Play Station 2 or a Game Boy. As a result, your parents and teachers may say, "You see, you can pay attention when you want to. You can play your Game Boy or

Nintendo for hours. Why can't you pay attention that well in school?" Of course our parents and teachers are often baffled by this seemingly contradictory behavior.

What many adults don't understand is that these electronic games are interactive and self-reinforcing—in other words, these gadgets are the perfect teaching tools for someone with ADD or ADHD. They're fun, interesting and hands-on. And you know immediately if you have played the game right. Unfortunately, few activities at school or chores at home provide this same ideal learning situation.

Here is another surprising fact; experts say that it's not so much that we're easily distracted, but rather that we're actually drawn to more interesting, rewarding, and fun activities or information. Our brains *require* and are always looking for more interesting stimulation in order for us to pay attention. So you see, it's not as simple as just telling us to pay attention. Most of us would like to pay attention rather than constantly fight with our parents and teachers, but our brains just don't always cooperate.

Paying Attention

Obviously, most all of us have problems listening and paying attention in a lot of situations. At school, I had a terrible time listening to my teachers before I started taking my medicine. Sometimes I just sat, stared off into space, and daydreamed. Frequently, I didn't hear my parents when they were talking to me. Most of the time, I didn't ignore them on purpose.

If you have ADD or ADHD, you may make what seem like careless errors in your schoolwork since it's very difficult for you to pay attention to details. You may make simple addition and subtraction errors in math or overlook spelling and grammatical errors.

Advice on Paying Attention

Alex's Advice:

> **Know your "listening limits."** Figure out what your listening limits are. Discuss them with your parents. When you feel like you can't listen anymore and find yourself drifting, tell your parents, "I'm sorry. Can we stop for a minute? My meds are gone and I can't pay attention." If your parents start a sentence and are halfway through it before you even realize that they're talking,

that's a clear sign that you have reached your "listening limits."

➢ **Talk with your parents.** Make certain your parents are aware that your listening limit is only five to ten minutes. It will also help if you agree upon a key word or signal such as having them tap you on the shoulder to get your attention first. Then they should sit face to face, eye to eye when talking with you.

➢ **Consider medicine.** The most important action I take to help me pay attention better is to take my Adderall XR. But taking medication *will not* make you pay attention; you still have to want to listen and really work at it. You must learn some tricks to help yourself pay attention.

  ➢ **Work at paying attention.** First, I constantly had to be aware and remind myself to jump right back in and listen to the teacher when my mind wandered. The good news is that taking medicine makes it so much easier for me to listen to the teacher.

  ➢ **Take notes.** Taking notes may help some, but don't slip into just doodling.

  ➢ **Sit up front.** Some students prefer to sit up front so that there are fewer distractions. However, I learned to pay attention even when I sat at the back of the room. Thanks to the Z in Zeigler, the teacher usually put me near the back of the room anyway.

  ➢ **Ask for a note taker.** Some of us are eligible to have a note taker as part of our IEP or Section 504 Plan. Typically, this is a good accommodation for many of us who have problems with taking good notes.

  ➢ **Get teacher notes.** When I was in college, occasionally I asked for my teacher's lecture notes ahead of time. I looked over them before class, so that I knew what to expect. It was easier to pay attention and even if my mind wandered, it was easier to get back into the lecture.

Ari's Advice:

➢ **Consider medication.** Taking medicine helps me pay attention the best.

➢ **Take notes.** Taking notes also keeps me focused and helps me pay attention better.

Erik's Advice:

➢ **Consider medicine.** I have a daily routine: I take Concerta every morning before school and that really helps me to pay attention. If I forget to take it, then I've noticed that my behavior is not as good. Right now I also take Paxil each day. I haven't had any problems with side effects.

Kyle's Advice:

➤ **Ask your mom to help.** When my mind drifts, my mom stops talking mid-sentence and then slows down her speech until I can get back on track.

Nathan's Advice:

➤ **Keep your hands busy.** Sometimes at church I have trouble sitting still. I found out that if I play with something with my hands, like Silly Putty or an eraser, that I can actually listen to the preacher during his sermon.

Khris's Advice:

➤ **Ask a friend to help.** I asked a good friend who sits near me to tap me on the shoulder to remind me to pay attention. To me, that's so much better than the embarrassment of having the teacher remind me to concentrate.

Jeremy's Advice:

➤ **Take notes.** A teacher taught me a great way to take notes. You classify and organize things as you go along. I have to concentrate so hard to take notes this way that it helps me to pay attention. I take notes in an outline form that reminds me of a stepladder. I put Roman numerals by the most important things. Then I make notes of any related topics with regular numbers, capital and then small letters.

Kati's Advice:

➤ **Tell teachers that active teaching strategies help.** It's really hard for me to pay attention in a class where the teacher just lectures. I do better in classes where the teacher uses overheads and groups for project learning. Using a laptop also helps because I can take notes faster. Perhaps you or your parents can tell your teacher that you learn better with hands-on, interactive, visual teaching strategies.

Paying Attention when You Drive

Distractions can be dangerous! Once when I was driving to my summer job, before my medicine kicked in, I bent over to pick up something I dropped and drove my car into a huge brick mailbox. The car was totaled. I was just sick; I loved my Firebird.

Alex's Advice on Driving Safely

- **Medication helps.** Although I'm a good driver, I tend to drive too fast. Taking medicine really helps me pay attention while I'm driving and that means I'm a safer driver. I'm working on driving more slowly.
- **Take driver's training.** I took driver's training at my high school and I thought it was really helpful.
- **Don't pack your car with friends.** Experts say that the more people you have in the car, the more likely you are to be distracted and have an accident. For more comments on driving, see "Driving & Attention Deficits" in Chapter 3, Coping with ADD and ADHD.

Absent-minded Professor

(forgetfulness)

You know you have an attention deficit if...

⇒ You frequently forget your homework assignments and books, regardless of how many times your parents and teachers remind you.

⇒ You remember you have a test when you walk into class and see everyone else studying.

⇒ Instead of asking how your day went, your mother greets you at the door by asking, "Did you remember your homework assignments and books?"

⇒ You studied the night before, but when the test starts you can't seem to remember anything.

⇒ You wake up and realize your big semester project is due today.

⇒ You're rich because your parents gave you a dollar for every homework assignment you've ever lost.

⇒ You hate to put things away because you can't remember where you put them.

Fact: Memory problems are a major characteristic of attention deficit disorder. So I'm sure it comes as no surprise to you that as a group, teenagers with ADD or ADHD are often extremely forgetful. We forget homework assignments, books, due dates for projects, and to stay after school for meetings, sports events, or even detention. In addition, we lose things. In fact, two of the official diagnostic characteristics of attention deficits are:

Forgetting Something?!

❶ "Is often forgetful in daily activities"

❷ "Often loses things necessary for tasks or activities"

Since these two problems are major characteristics, it's important for adults to realize that they must teach us new skills instead of just punishing us for our symptoms of ADD or ADHD. So, just like they teach a student with math deficits the skills to solve a math problem, they must teach new skills to students like us who are forgetful and disorganized so each of us can learn to compensate and remember our homework assignments! Because ADD and ADHD are disorders of forgetfulness, simply punishing us won't make these problems go away.

It's important to know about three types of memory and recall:

➤ *Short-term memory* usually means you can remember seven digits like a phone number for roughly twenty seconds.

➤ *Working memory* means you can hold information in your head while actively working on it, for example, thinking through a word problem in math.

➤ If you have problems with *working memory* that means you'll probably have trouble with *reading comprehension* or in other words, remembering important information that you have read. You may also have problems *summarizing or paraphrasing* what you read. Unfortunately, writing essays or reports is really hard for many of us.

➤ *Long-term memory* is where information is stored. *Recall* means quickly pulling information from its storage place in long-term memory.

Remembering Homework & Books

Right after school, I always had important things on my mind, like seeing my friends. When that last bell rang, I was so ready to leave school that I didn't want to fool with going back to my locker and getting my books.

Of course, after I got home, and when I did remember that I had homework, I couldn't remember what it was. Unfortunately, I knew that eventually my parents would make me do the work. Most of the time, one of my parents drove me back to school, or when I was older and could drive, they sent me back to get the books and assignments I needed. Luckily, my high school had night sessions, so we could usually find at least one door unlocked. When I was in college and took my medicine, I didn't have any major problems remembering my homework and books. Of course that may be because I didn't have a locker to leave them in.

Advice on Remembering Homework & Books

Well to be honest, this was always a hard one for me especially in high school. However, here are our best suggestions. Remember that you may be eligible to include some of the following tips as an accommodation in your IEP or Section 504 Plan.

Alex's Advice:

➤ **Develop a plan.** As I suggested in the section on disorganization, develop a system inside your locker to designate which books need to come home with you each day.

➤ **Use the school hotline or website.** Some schools also have a hot line or website that lists your assignments.

➤ **Call a classmate.** I also had a phone number for someone in most all of classes so I could call and ask for my assignments. Sometimes I even had to borrow a book from them.

➤ **Meet a teacher.** Although I never actually did this myself, some students have this included as part of their IEP or 504 Plan. You can meet with a teacher or teacher aide the last period of the day or right after school to review your specific homework assignments and books you need to take home.

  ➤ **Pay another student.** One mother paid a senior to meet her daughter after school so she would bring home all the right books and assignments

➤ **Use an electronic device.** My IPAC pocket PC is a huge help remembering important events. When I was in college I recorded test dates; now I list due dates for bills. It also has a built-in alarm reminder system that's really great.

Ari's Advice:

➤ **Use a planner.** My school gives every student a planner for recording assignments. Teachers write our homework on the board and then I have to write down the date, the subject and the assignments. If I forget my assignment, then I can always call a friend.

Tyler's Advice:

➤ **Take all your books home.** I take home all of my books every night and take back only the ones I need for school the next day. That way I always have the right books at home. I also try to remember to put all of the right books by the door at night so I'm organized for school the next morning.

➤ **Ask the teacher to e-mail assignments.** My teachers are pretty good about e-mailing all my assignments to us at home. This could be included as an accommodation in your IEP.

➤ **Ask for an extra set of books.** Fortunately, the school has given me an extra set of books to keep at home.

Kyle's Advice:

➤ **Do a mental checklist.** Each day after school, I go through this mental checklist about what my homework assignments are and which books I need. If I can't remember, I just ask a friend near my locker.

Kati's Advice:

➤ **Use electronic sticky notes.** I've started using electronic sticky notes on my laptop computer at school. That has really been helpful to me. You can download free software for these sticky notes from NetNote at www.alshare.com. I use the notes to remind me of things I have to do each day. For example, they can remind me to attend the extra "help class" that's offered right after lunch. I can even use different color notes for different subjects or activities I have to remember. My computer screen is set up with my notes along the lower right-hand corner of the screen.

➤ **Remember to backup your computer data.** Once, my laptop computer crashed and I lost everything. So be certain that you make back up copies of your work on the computer, just in case it crashes.

Perry's Advice:

➤ **Use a Palm Pilot.** My Palm Pilot has really been a lifesaver for me. In the past, I seemed to forget my homework assignments all the time or I would forget things I needed to do. Now I'm doing a much better job of remembering things.

Khris's Advice:

➤ **Use a Palm Pilot.** When I use my Palm Pilot, I not only can remember what my homework is, I can even remember to do it. Before I bought my Palm Pilot, I would forget due dates, a cover page, or put the assignment in a book bag or the wrong folder, and I would not find it until it was too late. So now, when the teacher writes the assignment on the board, I put the assignment and due date into my Palm Pilot right then. I put everything in my Palm Pilot!

Remembering Things My Parents Ask Me to Do

Sometimes when my parents asked me to do something like brush my teeth, I forgot it by the time I got to the bathroom. It's so easy for me to get distracted and interested in something else. And if it was something I hated, like cleaning up my room, I had a really hard time making myself get started on it.

Advice on Remembering Parental Requests

Alex's Advice:
➤ **Develop a routine.** Get into a routine for as many chores as possible. For example, each morning, brush your teeth right after you eat breakfast. Set your weekly medicine container next to your plate so you remember to take your medicine.
➤ **Make a list.** Ask your parents to write down two or three chores they want you to do. Mom usually put mine on the bathroom mirror. If you're embarrassed by it, then put the list somewhere so that your friends won't see it, like in a drawer near the sink. Of course, the whole point is if we don't see it, we'll never remember it. So if possible, keep the list out in plain sight.

Jeremy's Advice:
➤ **Do it now.** If my parents ask me to do something, I try to do it right away, because if I don't, I'll forget to do it at all.
➤ **Write things down.** Another tip is to put reminder notes where you can see them. One of my favorite places is on the door handle to my room. When I get up and open the door, I see the note right away. For example, if I forget to take out the trash, hopefully I'll see the note and remember that I need to do it immediately.

Losing Things

I've lost a lot of things over the years, like homework, books, clothes, shoes, coats, gloves, rings, wallets, money, watches, beepers, cell phones, and car keys. Sometimes I lay something down and forget where I put it. I've left my sunglasses in so many different places that I have to make myself put them in my pocket every time I go into a store.

Advice on Keeping Track of Things

Alex's Advice:
- **Knowing where things are.** I put my car keys in the same place every time I come home. This also works for books and assignments.
- **I.D. your stuff.** Don't forget to write your name and/or phone number on all your clothes, games, and CDs. That way if you lose them at least, someone will be able to return them to you.

Ari's Advice:
- **Have a back-up plan.**
  Sometimes I lose things, like my house key, but we have a back-up plan. My brother has a key and we've given one to our neighbor in case we get locked out of the house.

Khris's Advice:
- **Do homework on a computer.**
  I found it really helps to have my homework on my laptop computer. That way if I lose my homework or it gets all crumpled up I can transfer it onto a disk and print out another copy in the school library.

Memorizing Information

Memorizing information like multiplication tables or physics formulas or history facts is awfully hard for most of us. Even though we practiced my multiplication tables every night, I forgot them by the next day.

When it came to tests, I had trouble picking out the important information to study. And studying didn't always help because I forgot what I had studied by the time I took the test.

Advice on Studying & Memorizing Facts

Alex's Advice:

> **Ask for accommodations.** You may be eligible for certain accommodations, like using a calculator in math or a chart of formulas in algebra, chemistry or physics.

> **Use memory tricks.** Amelia gives you several memory tricks below. My mom also gives some suggestions in *Teaching Teens with ADD and ADHD.*

>> **Use mnemonics.** Use a mnemonic or memory trick like an acronym. Each letter in a common word stands for the items you're memorizing. One of the best known acronyms is *HOMES* for the great lakes—Huron, Ontario, Michigan, Erie and Superior.

>> **Use color.** Use color to highlight facts you need to remember or try color-coding materials. It's easier to remember words that are highlighted in pink or green rather than yellow.

Amelia's Advice:

> **Use visual posting.** At work, sometimes I tape my vocabulary list on the wall and memorize the words while I work the drive-through window. I also review them during slow times, like while I'm making the bread sticks.

> **Use acrostics.** Memorizing anything in math is so hard for me that even though I passed Algebra I and II in high school, I couldn't learn my multiplication tables. To help me remember the metric system, I used an acrostic for the metric units—kilo, hecto, etc: *King Henry Died Monday Drinking Chocolate Milk!*

Katie's Advice:

> **Use flash cards.** Sometimes we put facts I have to memorize on flash cards. For example, one time we put the names of the states and capitals on them.

Kati's Advice:

> **Ask for a study guide.** I often ask my teachers for study sheets before a big exam. These guides help us by identifying the major points to study.

Ready...<u>Fire</u>...Aim...Oops!

(impulsivity)

You know you have an attention deficit if...

⇒ Vacuuming the water out of the toilet seemed like a good idea at the time.

⇒ As a child, you took a note home to your parents inviting them to come to school the next morning. "Sorry Dad, my principal wants to talk to you. She wasn't very happy when I was break-dancing on the hood of her car."

⇒ Your motto is, "NO FEAR!" and you'll try almost anything once.

⇒ You find yourself saying, "But officer, I didn't know it was against the law to dive off this bridge. What do you mean you're giving me a ticket?"

⇒ Your first time snow skiing you don't wait for any lessons. You ski straight down the steepest slope only to be stopped by the ski patrol for speeding.

⇒ You join and quit activities or relationships at Mach speed—karate, Scouts, sports, boyfriends or girlfriends.

Fact: Being impulsive is another one of the key characteristics of ADHD and to a lesser degree, ADD inattentive. Impulsivity may be observed in schoolwork or in the things teens say or do. If you have ADHD, you may impulsively rush through your work and put down the first answer that comes into your head. Another example of impulsivity is quickly marking a multiple-choice test after reading the first answer and not reading the other answers carefully. You may also fail to double-check your answers on homework or tests and are more likely to blurt out answers and interrupt people who are talking. Taking shortcuts when doing schoolwork is another sign of impulsivity.

Although impulsivity is not listed as a characteristic of ADD inattentive, teens with this type of attention deficit certainly can be

*The term "Ready, Fire, Aim, Oops!" is quoted from *Teaching the Tiger* by Pruitt & Dornbush.

impulsive at times. For example, we're often impulsive when it comes to spending money. It seems like money burns a hole in our pocket; if we have it, we spend it. This is the reason adults may say we have trouble delaying gratification. We hate waiting to do anything so we pester our parents relentlessly to go to the store NOW so we can spend our money on a new game or CD!

To be effective, rewards must be given pretty quickly, typically within a week or so. That's why being told that we'll get a special reward if we make all A's typically doesn't motivate us. Even though we want to do well in school, rewards that happen too far in the future (usually eight weeks away) won't motivate us to make good grades.

Some teens with either ADD or ADHD are daring and take unnecessary risks. Occasionally, we get caught up in the emotions of the "moment" and act impulsively, for example skipping school, shoplifting on a dare, or jumping off high cliffs or a bridge into a lake. It's only after the fact that we stop to think about the risk or the consequences. Researchers tell us that some teens also inherit a gene that is linked to daring behavior.

Sometimes we don't think about the consequences until we're caught doing something wrong by school officials or law enforcement officers. Typically we don't attempt to hide or cover up our actions because we don't always realize that we're doing something wrong. Consequently, we're more likely to be caught misbehaving. True to form, we're so impulsive that we don't even plan ahead to avoid getting caught.

Students with attention deficits may misbehave, be punished and then repeat the same misbehavior. When I was younger, I really felt badly about doing that. Repeating misbehavior always baffles our parents and is often confusing to us too. You really do want to behave and keep your parents happy. However, experts tell us that students with attention deficits don't learn from punishments and rewards as easily as other teens. It seems that we lack the split second ability to stop and think, "Now, I'd better not do this or I'll be in deep trouble." We often act first, and then think, "Oh boy, I shouldn't have done that!" We often regret what we did, but we can't take it back.

Impulsive Spending

Although I don't rush through my schoolwork, blurt out answers, or interrupt people when they're talking, I'm impulsive when it comes to spending money. I can't resist buying new electronic gadgets.

Advice on Money Management

Alex's Advice:

> **Spend wisely.** Talk about your spending habits with your parents and work together to come up with a plan or develop a budget. If you're trying to save money, you may ask them to keep some of your allowance and put it into a savings account.

> **Avoid credit card misery.** When you move out on your own or leave for college, there are some steps you can take to reduce impulsive spending with a credit card. Don't carry the card in your wallet: leave it at home in a safe place so you can't buy anything impulsively. Here is a tip I picked up from a radio talk show host: put the card in a baggie with water and freeze it; then you have to plan ahead to use it.

Nathan's Advice:

> **Save part of your allowance.** When my sister and I get our allowance, our parents put half of it in savings for us. We also give some to the church and the rest of it is ours to spend. If there is something really special I want to buy, my parents will consider letting me spend my savings. It makes me think twice about asking my parents to buy me something if I have to spend part of my savings to get it. I can make extra money if I mow the yard, but I still have to put part of it into savings.

Perry's Advice:

> **Don't carry much cash.** It's much too easy to spend cash if you're carrying it with you.

> **Use a special bank card.** Although I don't have a checking or savings account, I give my checks to my parents and they put a limited amount of money on my special bank card. Basically that means they can control which stores I can use and the kinds of stuff I can buy. Typically, they transfer money from their checking account to my

account, but if they need to they can also transfer money from a credit card.

> **Consider a debit card.** A debit card allows you to spend based upon how much money you have in your checking account. Unlike a credit card, you can't spend more money than you have in your account. If your try to use your card when your money is too low, they won't approve your purchase.

Saying Things Without Thinking, Being Daring, & Getting into Trouble

I'm not a big talker, but when I was younger, I had trouble keeping secrets. Once when my dad told me what he bought a friend for Christmas, I got all excited and told her. He was really angry and spanked me.

As a child, I was known as a daredevil. I would try almost anything at least once. During the summers, our greatest adventure was to ride our bicycles down the sidewalk, across the dock, up the ramp and then do a one and a half dive over the handlebars into the lake. (See the picture on the cover of the book.) The only person who ever got hurt was someone who didn't have an attention deficit. My friend was too cautious and slow; it took seven stitches to sew up the gash in his leg.

Advice on Being Less Impulsive

Alex's Advice:

> **Consider medication.** Really the best thing I do to be less impulsive is to take my medicine. It gives me time to think about the risks and consequences of my decisions to do daring things before I act.

> **Accept compromise.** Sometimes the activities I wanted to try were pretty dangerous and my parents would set limits. For example, when I rode my bicycle off the ramp into the lake, I had to agree to reduce the height of the ramp. Otherwise, it pitched me almost straight up into the air and I might have landed in shallow water or on top of the ramp.

Jeremy's Advice:

> **Consider medication.** In the past, I said things without thinking and sometimes that got me into trouble. Now that I take

Adderall XR and Prozac, my moods are a lot better and I can actually stop and think before I say something. I feel better. The medicines help calm me down and I'm not so quick to get angry. I find that I'm not so edgy and not so quick to jump to the wrong conclusions when someone says something.

Khris's Advice:

➢ **Getting older helps.** As I've gotten older, I've out grown some of my impulsive behaviors. For example, when I was small, I threw little balls of wet toilet paper on the ceiling in the school bathroom and they stuck up there. I saw someone else do it and I thought it looked like fun.

Kati's Advice:

➢ **Ask mom for cues.** Sometimes my mother also helps me in social situations by giving me cues so that I avoid saying something impulsively. She may give me a certain look or nudge me.

➢ **Consider taking medication.** One of the most important things I do to help control my impulsivity is to take my medication. When I take my meds, I can remember to think before I act...most of the time. But I have to admit that even with my medicine, sometimes I'm still impulsive.

When I take my medicine, it's easier to be more thoughtful around my friends. For example, if one of my friends says something weird, instead of saying, "Oh, that's weird!" I stop and think, "What if it were me in that position? Would I want someone to say that to me? How would it make me feel?"

Adrian's Advice:

➢ **Be your own person.** Don't let other people influence you to do things that might seem like fun now but that you might regret later. When I was younger and got bored, I did things that got me in trouble. But I don't do that anymore. It's always best to be your own person and think for yourself.

"I'm Late for...Everything!"

(can't accurately judge the passage of time)

You know you have an attention deficit if...

⇒ "Be there in ten minutes" really means you'll be there in an hour—if your parents are lucky.

⇒ Your whole family is sitting in the car with the motor running, waiting for you.

⇒ Your favorite question on long trips is, "Are we there yet?"

⇒ Your parents say you'll be late to your own funeral.

⇒ You're on a first name basis with the secretary at school who checks in late students.

⇒ When you tell friends what time you'll meet them, they automatically:

   ⓐ   Multiply it by 3.

   ⓑ   Add one hour.

   ⓒ   Don't expect to see you at all.

⇒ You think planning ahead means what you'll do fifteen minutes from now.

⇒ You hyperfocus and lose track of time when you're on the computer. One minute it's noon and the next minute it's dark.

Fact: Most students with ADD and ADHD have trouble accurately judging the passage of time. Researchers have found that we're often late because we have a very *poor sense of time*. In one study, students with attention deficits couldn't accurately *measure* ten-second time intervals, yet students who didn't have attention deficits could do this correctly. We also have trouble *estimating* time, for example guessing how long it will take us to do our homework. That may be one reason we avoid our homework; it feels like it will take forever, partly because we can't measure time accurately.

Dr. Anne Welch, a veteran teacher, explains that our attention deficit often "robs us of our ability to use time wisely." Our disability "steals precious minutes and hours each day" which makes it much harder to get things done.

Because a good sense of time is necessary to plan ahead, we don't plan ahead very well. Instead we may put off major projects until the night before they're due. Experts tell us that the neurotransmitter, *dopamine*, must be working properly in order for us to accurately judge time.

Students with an attention deficit are often described as living in the "here and now." It's as though everything is today; there is no tomorrow. In fact, researchers found that unlike our friends, we tend to talk about today rather than next week, next month or next year. That means we don't plan for the future very well. Consequently, most of us need guidance and support if we are to plan adequately for the future.

Time Awareness

I really don't want to be late—it just seems like I can't get organized so I can leave on time.

> **For school.** When I was in high school, I was always late getting to school mainly because my high school classes started so early—at 7:20. I had a terrible time waking up, getting dressed and organized, and leaving on time. I did much better when I was in college and could schedule my classes later in the morning.

> **For family activities.** When we went somewhere, I was usually the last one ready and every one else had to wait for me. I was also late for dinner a lot and that didn't make my mother very happy.

> **For activities with friends.** I had trouble coming home on time when I went out with friends and regularly missed my curfew.

Advice on Being on Time

Alex's Advice:

> **Set all of your clocks ahead by ten minutes.** However, you have to be careful. When you know the clock is ten minutes fast, you may simply slow down and still be late.

> **Ask someone to give you a reminder.** Sometimes my parents warned me when I had ten minutes left before we had to leave for school.

> **Use a wristwatch alarm.** In high school, I had a wristwatch with

an alarm that beeped to remind me when I had to take my medicine or turn in a report.

- **Use a beeper.** My parents got tired of grounding me when I came home late, so we finally decided that they could beep me fifteen minutes before I was due home.
    - My parents and I also developed a code so that they could beep me to remind me to take my medicine. We used my birth date, 526, as the code. Recently, I heard about a college that beeps students to remind them to leave for class or begin their regularly scheduled study time.
- **Use a cell phone.** When I was in college, people called me on my cell phone to remind me to meet them.
- **Practice time estimation.** As you start your homework, write down how long you think it will take to finish your work. Then compare it with how long it actually took to complete. It may not take as long as you think it will.

Tyler's Advice:

- **Wake up early.** I'm more likely to get to school on time if I get up on time. So my parents wake me half an hour early and give me my morning dose of medicine (20 mgs of Ritalin and 20 mgs of Ritalin SR). Then when I do get up, I'm more alert, able to function, and can get ready for school on time.

Khris's Advice:

- **Use a Palm Pilot.** My Palm Pilot beeps and vibrates to remind me when and where I need to be. When my band is playing somewhere, we have to be there an hour early to get set up and have time to warm up. When I get up in the morning, I set my Palm Pilot to remind me two hours before and one hour before I need to be at a gig.
- **Consider programming a cell phone.** Some students might program their cell phones to remind them what time they need to be somewhere. They can set it to vibrate so that it doesn't disturb anyone.

Jeremy's Advice:

- **Get your medicine right.** Last year I was late to school a lot—52 tardies. But this year, I have finally gotten my medication right and getting to school on time has not been a major problem. I had such terrible sleep problems that I couldn't wake up and get to school on time.

➤ **Go to bed on time.** Now I plan to go to bed by 10:30 or 11:00 so I can get enough sleep. My doctor also prescribed some medication to help me fall asleep.

Getting Things Done on Time

Perry explains that adults should not assume that someone who wants to be better at time management can just do it automatically. After all, time is an abstract concept, so you need a reminder that you can see or hear, like a list of chores or an alarm on a timer.

Advice on Getting Things Done on Time

Alex's Advice:

➤ **Make yourself more aware of time.** Consider buying a special timer that shows the red portion disappearing as time passes. By doing this, you're making time, an abstract concept, visible so you can actually "see" it pass. Visit www.timetimer.com for more information.

Perry's Advice:

➤ **Use a Palm Pilot.** I always put my "to do list" in my Palm Pilot. That helps me get my schoolwork and chores done.

Impact of Time Awareness on Driving

I'm always running late because I never seem to allow enough "get ready" time and I often underestimate how much travel time I need. For example, I often estimate travel time using the fastest time I've ever made the trip, like when there was no traffic, which means I only allow twenty minutes when I should have allowed thirty. Then I try to make up the time by driving over the speed limit, which usually gets me into a lot of trouble.

Advice on Arriving on Time

Alex's Advice:

➤ **Add in travel, get ready, and "Oops!" time**, when you go somewhere. For example, if you have to be at school at 7:20, then allow enough time for the ride to school, say twenty minutes or so, then add extra time for getting your clothes and books together and getting in the car, maybe ten minutes. Next, add fifteen minutes to find a parking place, get your books, go by your locker, and walk to class. You should add another five to ten minutes of "oops!" time because you probably underestimated how much time you needed.

You might talk this through with your parents to make sure you allow enough extra time to make it to school on time. You may also get help from other adults—maybe a guidance counselor, a relative, a coach, or someone at your church or synagogue.

Planning for the Future

Although I have good intentions, most of the time I need reminders about planning for the future. For example, when I graduated from high school, I wanted to go to college, but I couldn't get organized enough to fill out the required paperwork.

Advice for Planning Ahead

Alex's Advice:

➤ **Ask for help.** Although I hate to admit it, I had to ask for help with the paper work for college. Finally I gave my parents permission to fill out the forms. I signed them and then my parents mailed them for me. Most teenagers with ADD or ADHD need help planning for the future. So let your parents or other adults help you with this process. Eventually, as you get older and with continued practice, you'll get better at planning ahead on your own.

➤ **Ask for a good "transition plan" as part of your IEP.** As part of an IEP (Individualized Educational Program) federal education law requires that beginning at age fourteen, teachers are supposed to help you develop a "transition plan" for what you're going to do after you graduate from high school. You might do an internship or work with a mentor in a career that's interesting to you, like programming computers.

Night Owls & Morning Zombies

(can't fall asleep or wake up easily)

You know you have an attention deficit if…

⇒ You get into bed and you can't fall asleep. You may lie there for hours, tossing and turning.

⇒ You're a night owl. Sometimes your sleep schedule seems to be the opposite of the rest of the world's. You're ready to go to sleep when everyone else seems to be waking up.

⇒ If you have ADHD, your body is going a hundred miles an hour, but you're afraid to sit down because if you slow down, you'll fall asleep.

⇒ You sleep soundly—like a dead person. You once slept through an earthquake that measured 5.0 on the Richter scale.

⇒ Sometimes your parents wake you up for school and you talk with them, but a half an hour later, you can't remember the conversation.

⇒ Your father has gotten so frustrated that he has threatened to pour water on you to wake you up.

Fact: Fifty percent of all teenagers with attention deficits have trouble falling asleep and waking up. Certain chemicals in the brain allow most teenagers to fall asleep and wake up more easily. *Serotonin*, a brain neurotransmitter, has a major impact on our ability to get restful sleep. That means if the chemicals in your brain are not right, even if you go to bed on time, you can't fall asleep. Some of us also have *delayed sleep cycles*. Unfortunately, most of the time we can't get away with sleeping from 4:00 a.m. until noon.

When your brain chemicals aren't working right, you won't get restful sleep. You may wake up tired, even after getting eight hours of sleep, and that may be why you sleep in class sometimes.

Levels of serotonin must be high enough for teenagers and adults to get restful sleep. During an average night, there are about six cycles of deep sleep. One deep sleep cycle is called *slow wave (SW) sleep* and the other is called *REM sleep.* REM refers to the rapid eye movements that occur during this period. Most of your dreams occur during REM. Experts tell us that both deep sleep cycles play a critical role in learning and memory. So as you can see, getting restful sleep is critical, especially for us, since we often have trouble memorizing information.

Everyone knows that if you take medication too late in the day, it makes it harder for you to fall asleep. Here is an important fact: sometimes parents mistakenly assume that ADD and ADHD medications alone cause your sleep problems. But as you can see, your sleep problems are often totally unrelated to your medicine.

Sleep Problems

I have trouble going into and out of my sleep cycles. My body is ready to go to sleep, but my mind can't relax.

> **Falling asleep.** At night I lose track of time and before I know it, it's midnight. Even when I get into bed, it's like I can't turn off my mind. It jumps from one idea to the next. Usually I'm thinking about something that I have to do the next day, regardless of whether I'm excited about it or dreading it.

Advice on Getting Restful Sleep

Alex's Advice:

> **Develop a good sleep routine.** I take a nice hot soaking bath and maybe drink a glass of milk near bedtime. One of the reasons I drink milk is that it contains melatonin, which generates serotonin that can help with sleep. Find something that helps you relax and do this every night before you go to bed. Sometimes music works for me. Eventually your body will begin to associate what you're doing during relaxation time with sleep.

> **Talk with your doctor** if you have serious problems getting to sleep. He or she may suggest a sleep evaluation or suggest a new medication. Clonidine or Trazadone are two medications that doctors sometimes use to help with sleep.

>> **Consider other medication options.** When I was younger, my doctor told me that taking Benadryl at night might help me sleep. However, don't take it every night—experts tell

us that taking it too often can make your memory worse. When I was in college, I took melatonin sublingual which means it dissolves in my mouth. **Caution:** You should not take any medications, prescription or over-the-counter, unless you talk with your doctor first.

➤ **Wear yourself out.** Exercise on a regular basis, just not near bedtime. Look for activities that wear you out. For example, I discovered that spending time in the sun while playing basketball or riding a jet ski seems to wear me out.

Katie's Advice:

➤ **Consider medication.** I have some pretty bad sleep problems, so I take clonidine before bedtime to help me fall asleep and sleep more deeply.

Tyler's Advice:

➤ **Consider medication.** I also take clonidine at night to help me sleep. Otherwise I can't fall asleep and I'll be up all night.

Kati's Advice:

➤ **Consider taking medicine.** I've found that Seroquel helps me fall asleep more easily at night. If not, when I get in bed, I fidget and toss and turn a lot. It may take me two or three hours to fall asleep. Sometimes if I can't sleep, I get up and go downstairs and watch TV until I get sleepy.

Jeremy's Advice:

➤ **Consider medication.** Since I started taking Zyprexa, I can actually fall asleep when I get in bed. Before I began taking medicine, I would go to bed on time, but I just couldn't fall asleep.

➤ **Take your medicine on time.** If I take my Adderall XR too late in the day, then I can't fall asleep at night. For example, I usually take it no later than 7:00 a.m.

Getting Up on Time

When I was in high school, I had a terrible problem getting up on time. My alarm would go off and I would never hear it. My parents and I had terrible fights every morning because I couldn't wake up on time.

Advice on Waking Up

Alex's Advice:

Everything is always worse when I don't get up on time. My day gets off to a really bad start. So here are some of my favorite ideas to help me get up on time.

- **Set two radio alarm clocks**.
  - Set one for when you want to get up ideally.
  - Set the second one for when you absolutely have to get up.
  - Set one on a different music station that you hate so you'll want to get up to turn it off. Country music does the trick for me!
- **Put one clock across the room** and set the alarm, not just the "wake to music" button.
- **Buy a loud alarm clock.** We found an alarm that truckers use called a *Screaming Meanie.* It doesn't look like a clock; instead you set a timer to go off in a certain number of hours. It sounds like a siren. You can find several loud alarm clocks at big "truck stop plazas."
  - On a regular alarm clock, turn the volume up as loud as possible.
- **Be creative—find a good reason to wake up.** For example, have your girlfriend or someone special call to wake you up each morning. Or record your own voice on a tape recorder, plug it into a timer, and wake yourself up.

Aaron's Advice:

- **Watch a favorite TV program.** The perfect way to wake me up each morning is to watch "Starship Troopers" while I get ready for school.

Tyler's Advice:

- **Wake up early.** As I explained earlier, it's easier for me to get up and get ready for school if my parents wake me thirty minutes early and give me five milligrams of Ritalin. Then I go back to sleep. When I wake up the second time, my medicine has kicked in, and I can wake up more easily. Plus I'm in a better mood.

Jeremy's Advice:

- **Set an alarm.** I set my alarm and turn the music up really loud. I set the alarm fifteen minutes early to allow myself just a few more minutes of sleep. When the alarm goes off a second time,

I know I have to get right up or I'll be late getting to school.

➤ **Ask for help.** I've asked my mother to come and wake me up if I don't get up after the second alarm.

Amelia's Advice:

➤ **Exercise.** I usually exercise earlier in the day so that I increase my endorphins (brain chemicals that give me a "natural high") and I feel better. This has really helped me.

➤ **Schedule classes later.** Getting up early is still really hard for me. I had to drop my early morning volleyball class this semester because I just couldn't wake up. You might schedule classes later if possible.

➤ **Ask for help.** I'm lucky because my roommate is very understanding and helps me wake up.

Hieroglyphics & Doodling 101

(messy handwriting & printing)

You know you have an attention deficit if...

⇒ Your handwriting is so bad, you can't read your own writing.

⇒ Even if you do take notes; you can't read them.

⇒ Your parents tell you that with your handwriting that you could be a doctor someday.

⇒ You like to print much better than write cursive.

⇒ Your writing is a combination of half printing and half cursive.

⇒ You prefer to write with a mechanical pencil and you like pencil grippers.

Fact: The majority of teenagers with attention deficits have handwriting that's messy and difficult to read. Two or three problems seem to make handwriting harder for us—poor fine motor coordination, limited working memory capacity, and slow processing speed. Simply stated, your memory capacity is smaller, your fingers often don't work as well as they should, and you often do school work more slowly than your friends.

Since many teens have poor fine motor coordination skills, they often prefer to print, or write using a combination of printing and cursive. My mom has made an interesting observation: sometimes we have good reasons for the things we do, although it may not be obvious at the time. For example, you may prefer to print because it's easier; it actually requires less memory than writing cursive. Because handwriting is often slow and requires a lot of effort, you may hate to write and may be more likely to avoid your homework.

Copying from the board is also difficult because it takes so much time and effort. Copying from the board and remembering information both require good working memory. Since our memory capacity is limited, the chunks of information we can hold in our minds at one time are smaller. Consequently, it takes us longer to copy work from the board. Working memory and processing speed are important executive function skills.

Handwriting

I don't like to write and avoid it whenever I can. I tend to write more slowly than other students. Writing is hard for me. I still prefer to print even though I'm an adult now.

➤ **Printing vs. cursive.** I always liked to print instead of writing in cursive. First teachers taught me how to print, and then they wanted me to change all that and learn a new way to write— cursive. The way I see it, that's pretty dumb. That's just like learning to tie your shoes in a new way. I knew how to tie my shoes one way perfectly well, why would I want to learn to tie them another way.

Knowing how to print is in my subconscious: it's stored in my brain. I do it automatically. In fact, I can print faster than I write in cursive. My grandfather and aunt, who both have ADHD, do a combination of half printing and writing, the same way I do.

Finding the easiest way to do something is very important to me. I always take the quickest route between point A and B. Otherwise, I'm wasting time and energy.

➤ **Mechanical pencils.** I always liked writing with mechanical pencils. Maybe I feel like I have more control when I write with them.

➤ **Writing slowly.** When I was in the first grade my teacher made me write my whole name, Alexander, on all of my papers. I hated it! It took me so long to write my name that the rest of the class had almost finished the assignment before I completed my name.

Advice on Writing Problems

Alex's Advice:

➤ **Use a computer.** Computers really saved me. I was in the fourth grade when I started using a computer to do my schoolwork.

The good news is that a lot of schools now have computers or something like an *AlphaSmart*, which is a smaller inexpensive computer, for students to use. Since we're forgetful, the tricky part is figuring out a way to remember to take the computer to school and then bring it home. Maybe you can ask a friend to remind you to take it home everyday. You may even need to save everything on a disk or e-mail it home and leave the computer at school. Definitely put your name on the computer; you don't want to lose it.

> **Use a keyboard with your IPAQ.** A lot of pocket PCs like an IPAQ or Palm Pilot also have keyboards so you can take notes at school.

> **Ask for accommodations at school.** If you have ADD or ADHD, slow reading and writing, and bad handwriting that slows you down, you may be eligible for accommodations on your IEP or Section 504 Plan. These accommodations, such as shorter assignments or extra time on written work and tests are very helpful. You may also ask for permission to do your schoolwork on the computer.

Perry's Advice:

> **Use a computer.** As part of my IEP, my school gives me a computer to use. Taking notes on a computer is much better because I can't read my own handwriting. Otherwise, taking notes really doesn't help me very much.

Keyboarding

I taught myself how to type and I'm pretty good at it. When I took keyboarding lessons in high school, I thought it would be a really easy class. But I was wrong. It was horrible; in fact, I hated the class. They wanted me to follow a particular format even though I could type faster using my method. Teachers always gave timed practice tests and that was a disaster for me; I was always very slow.

Advice on Keyboarding

Alex's Advice:

> **Take a keyboarding class.** If you're going to take a keyboarding class, take it when you're younger and first learning to type. We found a keyboarding program, *Type to Learn*, that should make

it easier. In some ways it may be good to avoid taking typing in high school. The timed tests are really a killer if you type a lot more slowly than your friends. If you do take a class in high school, just be aware that it may be frustrating.

➤ **Ask for accommodations in keyboarding class.** Your teacher may be willing to provide accommodations, such as shorter assignments or extra time.

Tyler's Advice:

➤ **Use a software program.** I learned to type faster by using a pretty good computer program called *Mavis Beacon Teaches Typing*. (Ari also used this program.)

A Tortoise or a Hare? ADD vs ADHD

(slow writing or rushing through work)

You know you have an attention deficit if...
⇒ You don't read the directions carefully before you start working.
⇒ You don't double-check your answers when you finish your homework or tests.

ADD
⇒ It takes you twice as long to finish homework as it takes other students.
⇒ You're still working on your test when all of your classmates have finished theirs.
⇒ You need something explained in several different ways before you can finally understand it.

ADHD
⇒ You mark the first answer you read on a multiple-choice test and don't read the other choices carefully.
⇒ You rush through your math test and are one of the first to finish. Later you realize that you skipped several key steps.

Fact: Many students with attention deficits, especially if you have ADD inattentive, read and write more slowly than students without attention deficits. This is often called *slow processing speed*. This tendency to read and write slowly also means that it will take us longer than it takes others to  do classwork and homework. In addition, you may have trouble with *recall*, which means you can't quickly find and remember facts that are stored in your *long-term memory*. So at times, you know the answer to a question, but just can't find it fast enough in your memory bank. This may be referred to as *slow retrieval of information*.

On the other hand, if you have ADHD, you may have exactly the opposite problem. You may rush through everything, not read instructions carefully, misread questions, and make careless errors on your homework and tests

Sometimes homework assignments cause problems because

they're too long. In fact, experts tell us that most teachers underestimate how long it will take students with learning problems and attention deficits to finish doing homework. Two national organizations, the Parent Teacher Association (PTA) and National Education Association (NEA) jointly recommend that students spend roughly ten minutes a night per grade on *all* homework—that means ninth graders would spend a total of around 90 minutes on homework for all their subjects.

Slow Writing Speed

I write more slowly than other students, so it always took me longer to do my schoolwork and homework. And, I was usually one of the last people to finish tests.

I knew it would take me such a long time to do my homework that I tried to avoid it as long as possible. I always hated doing it. Sometimes I would tell my parents that I didn't have any, even when I did. But somehow they always knew when I was being less than truthful. My parents monitored my homework very closely, especially if my grades were borderline.

Advice on Writing Speed & Homework

Alex's Advice:

> **Use a computer.** As mentioned earlier, computers can really help you write more information, more quickly.
> **Ask for accommodations at school.** If you read and write more slowly than most of your classmates, you'll probably be eligible for accommodations such as shorter homework assignments or extra time on tests.
> **Find out if the homework assignment is too long; reduce written work.** Mom told me about a good suggestion from Drs. Zentall and Goldstein. The teacher sends home a note stating how long the homework should take to complete. Parents and teens write down how long it actually took and then compare times. Next, review the PTA/NEA's guidelines in the "Facts" section and reduce the amount of homework if appropriate.

Ari's Advice:

> **Ask for extended time.** The accommodation that helps me the most is getting extra time for tests. I'm also eligible to use a

calculator and carry a chart with multiplication tables on it for math class.

Erik's Advice:

➤ **Get accommodations in your IEP.** When I was a freshman and sophomore in high school, I really needed several accommodations at school, such as assistance with writing, extra time on tests, and permission to redo or recopy assignments without being penalized. Fortunately, I don't need those extra supports now, but they're there if I need them.

Taking Notes

I really didn't take very good notes in high school. I spent a lot of time drawing and doodling. I've gotten better, but I still haven't perfected it. I tried taking shorthand, but I had trouble with it. My memory doesn't seem to work fast enough. I can't quickly remember the abbreviations, so I end up having to write all the words out. Actually, I have to think harder when I do shorthand. I have to think about the sentence and whether or not to leave out certain words. Personally, I could have actually written the whole sentence faster than writing it in shorthand.

Another problem I have with taking notes is that I'm a perfectionist. I have to write all of the words and they have to be spelled correctly. Sometimes I'm so focused on getting the words right that I'm not thinking about what they mean.

Advice on Note Taking

Alex's Advice:

➤ **Get a note taker.** Having someone else's notes was the perfect solution for me. That way I could listen to what the teacher said and think about what it meant. You can ask for a note taker as part of your IEP or 504 Plan. Or you can just ask a friend to give you a copy of his class notes.

➤ **Learn shorthand.** If you don't have major problems with your working memory, you may be successful taking shorthand. So learn some shorthand and see if it works for you. It will take a good bit of practice to get to the point where it becomes second nature. The symbols for shorthand, such as @ for at, T for the, and > for more than, are available in mom's book, *Teaching Teens with ADD and ADHD.*

➤ **Ask the teacher for a copy of her class notes.** Some teachers are willing to give you a copy of their notes. These can be very helpful for some students.

However, not every suggestion will work for every student. For example, getting the teacher's notes right before the lecture didn't always help me. I still had problems following along. I was too focused on the notes rather than listening to the teacher. I prefer to listen to the teacher and what she said in class. The visual cues from watching her write on the board, her comments and her body language made it easier to pick up on what was really most important. If I was busy looking over her notes, I would stare at my paper rather than looking at the teacher.

Tyler's Advice:

➤ **Taking notes.** When I get home from school, my mom types up my notes from class while I read them to her.

Careless Mistakes

Students with ADHD often rush through their schoolwork and make what teachers call, "careless mistakes" on schoolwork and tests. They just want to get their work done. At the time, it doesn't matter if it's right or wrong. For example, they may add all of the math problems because they're rushing so fast that they don't notice when the signs change from plus to minus or multiplication.

Advice on Working More Carefully

Ashley's Advice:

➤ **Use a highlighter.** My teacher taught us to read the directions for tests and worksheets carefully. Then we highlight the key words in the directions, especially verbs that are action words. She also has us highlight the math signs for each problem.

Brilliant Ideas Lost Forever

(problems writing essays & reports)

You know you have an attention deficit if...

⇒ Your ideal essay is short, maybe three sentences long.

⇒ You have fantastic, creative ideas but you can't get them out of your head and written down on paper.

⇒ You'd rather have your teeth drilled than revise a rough draft.

⇒ Your rough draft *is* the final copy.

Fact: One study reports that 65 percent of students with attention deficits have written expression problems. That means many of us will have trouble writing essays and reports, answering essay questions on tests, or responding to questions in class. In addition, it's also difficult for us to keep ideas in mind, remember them long enough to write them down, organize them in a logical sequence, and then remember all of the spelling and grammar rules. We may also have serious problems with our *working memory*— in other words, our ability to manipulate information in our head, organize it, and then remember it long enough to write it down. Writing is another skill that is dependent on good executive function skills, especially a good working memory. Experts also say that we may have trouble *selecting the main point* in material we read and have difficulty *summarizing* and *paraphrasing* material.

Writing Essays & Giving Speeches

➤ **Expressing myself.** Writing essays and giving speeches have always been hard for me. Of course, this is not true for everyone with an attention deficit, but I avoid both situations like the plague.

➤ **Teacher feedback.** Sometimes I turned in a paper and thought it was pretty good and the teacher wrote red marks all over it. You get hesitant to write after that because you're afraid that it's bad.

➤ **Writing essays or reports.** It's easier to write about subjects I'm familiar with. If I don't know much about a topic, it's hard to write several paragraphs. In a way it's like giving a speech, except in this case I feel like everyone is staring at my words. I don't want to look bad or have someone laugh at what I've written because they think it's stupid.

➤ **Getting my ideas organized.** I have trouble putting my ideas together and organizing them. Sometimes I have these great ideas but it's so hard to put them down on paper. It's as though I don't know what to do with my ideas. It helps if I have a plan and know how to put my ideas in order. I also find it easier to tell someone what I'm thinking rather than trying to write down my ideas.

➤ **Remembering my ideas.** I hated writing essays for class. Even when I was a senior in college, it was so hard to capture all the ideas in my head. My words on paper are never the same as my thoughts because I can't remember what I was thinking. When I start writing my thoughts on paper, I only get part of them because I write so much more slowly than I think. By the time I finish writing the first sentence, I skip the middle sentence because my thoughts have already started on the last sentence. For example, if I had not dictated this to someone, my original thoughts would probably look more like this: "When I'm writing my ideas on paper, I don't get all of them because my mind is already on the last sentence." So my five sentence paragraph suddenly becomes only one sentence.

Advice on Writing Essays

Alex's Advice:

➤ **Dictate to someone.** I often dictated my essays to one of my parents. Typically, my mom typed it up and then I edited, cut and pasted it on my computer. You can also dictate to a friend, classmate, or a teacher's aide.

➤ **Use a graphic organizer.** Graphic organizers can also be very helpful. Organizers give you a template or layout to follow so you don't have to worry about remembering the rules for writing an essay. In fact, there is an organizer for writing essays in Appendix 9.

➤ **Brainstorm and write down ideas.** You can write your ideas on Post-it notes and rearrange them as to how they should flow in an essay.

Amelia's Advice:

➤ **Use a computer.** Using a computer helps a lot. I also look for a webpage with synonyms or a thesaurus. To give me structure, I have a general outline in my head that I follow when I'm writing. It's something like using the graphic organizer in this book.

➤ **Write neatly.** I also print in all caps because it helps me write more neatly.

Erik's Advice:

➤ **Ask for help on the draft.** I have learned to write a draft and then show it to the teacher before it's due. Most of the time, she will point out some words or punctuation I should change. Then I get one of my parents to read my report and also make suggestions. If I make those changes, then my final draft usually turns out to be pretty good.

Ari's Advice:

➤ **Use computer software.** I like to use *Inspiration*, a computer software program, to help with my writing.

Kyle's Advice:

➤ **Design your own graphic organizer.** My teacher gave me an easy graphic organizer and I created my own for my computer. I tried using a "web," which is a drawing with

lines coming out from the center to show how ideas are related to each other. But it only confused and frustrated me.

Ari's Advice:

➤ **Write about topics you know.** Hopefully, you'll be allowed to select a topic that's especially interesting to you. For me those topics would be scuba diving, skateboarding, snowboarding, and wakeboarding.

Writing Short Essays

When I write, I'm direct and like to get to the bottom line. I use the least number of words possible. Unfortunately, my teachers didn't like my approach; they told me my essays were too short.

➤ **Research papers.** It's extra hard for me to research a topic, understand it, and then write about it. Even if I do research an issue, I feel uneasy or unsure about what I'm writing because I don't fully understand it. It's harder for me to learn by just reading about something. I need to see or work with it firsthand.

➤ **Perfectionism.** Another part of my problem is perfectionism. I don't want to turn in a paper that is not perfect, but I can't finish writing an essay in a fifty minute class. It takes me much longer than that because I just can't capture all my ideas in a rough draft. For some reason, I can't begin on the next paragraph until each section is corrected.

Advice on Writing Longer Essays

Alex's Advice:

➤ **Ask for extended time.** If you're eligible, ask for extended time for writing essays. Include this accommodation in your IEP or Section 504 Plan.

➤ **Get a list of adjectives and adverbs.** One way to make the essay longer is to select adjectives and adverbs from a list and add them to the essay. Visit www.webster.commnet.edu for helpful lists and rules for adjectives and adverbs.

Summarizing & Paraphrasing

When I was in college I realized that I had trouble summarizing and paraphrasing, in other words picking out the main points and writing a summary without copying the old wording.

Advice on Paraphrasing

Kyle's Advice:

➣ **Practice paraphrasing.** My mother used information from encyclopedia software to teach me how to paraphrase. We highlight and copy a paragraph from the encyclopedia that summarizes the topic. Then we print it out triple spaced. Next I highlight the subject and verb. Then I write a new sentence using those key words. Of course we're careful not to plagiarize or copy the author's exact words.

Picking a Topic

I also had trouble picking a topic. Sometimes I would have a lot of topics to choose from but it was too hard to narrow them down—they were all equally bad. I could spend forty-five minutes just picking a topic. Other people could have written the whole essay by then.

Advice on Selecting a Topic

Alex's Advice:

➣ **Do a practice outline or essay.** If you can guess possible topics the teacher may pick, practice brainstorming ideas for the essay the night before.

➣ **Narrow your selection down.** When the teacher gives you several choices for an essay topic, quickly narrow them down. Write four topics on note cards, then narrow them to two topics, and then select the final one.

Remembering All the Rules

It's also really hard for me to write and also remember all of the grammar and spelling rules. When you have to worry about the rules, you lose your train of thought. You're concentrating so hard on writing correctly that you interrupt your creative thinking. Sometimes I would start writing and forget the idea I wanted to write down. I couldn't write the way I write best; that is taking my time, going back, and then correcting it. Clearly, just trying to remember all these rules puts a tremendous strain on our limited memory capacity.

Advice on Reducing the Memory Load

Alex's Advice:

➤ **Focus on one or two rules.** Coyle Bryan, a high school language arts teacher, focuses on only one or two key rules during each essay. For example, this week she may grade the essay for creative content and count off only for incomplete sentences or errors in subject and verb agreement. Next week she may focus on punctuation. Maybe your teacher will consider trying this strategy for the whole class.

➤ **Ask for two grades.** Consider including in the IEP or 504 Plan that the student will be given two grades: one for content and one for correct grammar. That way you're more likely to make a passing grade on an essay.

➤ **Ask for a graphic organizer.** Graphic organizers list the key parts of an essay so that you don't have to remember how to write a basic five-paragraph essay. If you have major memory problems, you could ask for a graphic organizer when you write an essay. This can also be written into your IEP/504 Plan.

Speaking in Class

Although I hated making presentations, I had to do it in a lot of my classes. When I was in high school, I once took an F rather than give a class presentation. I'm just not quick on my feet or witty like my friend Lewis, who was always the ADHD class clown. I have to fully understand something or I can't stand up and talk about it.

Sometimes when I sit and think too long about giving a speech, I convince myself that I can't do it. I get so anxious about speaking in class that, my throat gets dry, my voice changes, the room gets brighter, and I go blank. It's like I have an adrenaline rush and my brain overloads and shuts down. I'm always afraid I'll forget what I'm saying. I don't want to look stupid.

Advice on Speaking in Class

Alex's Advice:

> **Practice the night before.** One way to practice is to tell someone else about your topic to the point that they understand it too. Consider practicing in front of the mirror in your room, or in front of your parents.

> **Outline your speech on note cards.** It may help you to outline the key points of your speech and write them on note cards. That way you can glance at your notes to help trigger your memory.

> **Talk with your doctor.** If you have serious problems with anxiety when speaking in class, your doctor may consider prescribing a medication like Inderal.

Kyle's Advice:

> **Give a PowerPoint presentation.** PowerPoint presentations impress teachers. The slides help because you can see what comes next in your speech. (If you can't do a presentation from your computer, you can print out color PowerPoint transparencies and show them on an overhead projector.)

Remembering Two "F" Words:
Facts & Formulas

(difficulty with math)

You know you have an attention deficit if…

⇒ You've passed algebra, but you still don't know your multiplication tables.

⇒ You can figure out a way to get the right answer to a problem even though you don't do it exactly the way the teacher told you to do it.

⇒ Remembering math and physics formulas is a nightmare for you.

⇒ You write the numbers in your math problems very small, close together, and if possible on one line. You don't line up the columns very well and it's hard to know when you've made a mistake.

Fact: Many teenagers with attention deficits, especially the *inattentive* or *combined type*, have serious problems memorizing and quickly retrieving math facts such as multiplication tables, and addition and subtraction facts. We often can understand more difficult math concepts, but are slowed down when we actually work math or algebra problems and can't quickly recall our basic math facts. Remembering and quickly retrieving algebra, physics, or chemistry formulas from long-term memory are also very hard for us because these skills are dependent on good executive function skills.

Experts tell us that there are several reasons why math is so difficult for teens with attention deficits:

❶ It requires both reading and math skills which makes it more complex than just reading.

❷ It's hierarchical, meaning it builds on skills that you learned previously. Yet teachers may not give us enough time to master key concepts before moving on to new ones.

❸ Books are bigger and contain more concepts than can possibly be taught in the required 180 school days. Consequently, teachers are forced to introduce too many concepts too quickly.

❹ Memory and problem solving skills are critical but they are deficits for many of us who have ADD or ADHD.

Math

Math was always my worst subject.

➤ **Multiplication tables.** My parents and I practiced multiplication tables every night and I forgot them by the next morning.

➤ **Math/Algebra.** One of the major problems I had was that my teacher moved way too fast for me. I didn't want to speak up in high school because I was too embarrassed and didn't want to look dumb. I was afraid that people would make fun of me.

➤ **Algebra according to Alex.** The best way I learn is to take a problem, write it down, tear it apart and figure out how I got from point A to point B. I have my own way of figuring out problems. In fact when I was in high school, my parents kidded me that I did "algebra according to Alex." I drove my teachers crazy because I could get the answer right, but I didn't always do problems the way they said to do them.

➤ **Calculus.** Although I barely passed high school and college algebra, I managed to make an A in college calculus and even ended up with a 100 average in the class.

Advice on Improving Your Math Grades

Alex's Advice:

➤ **Use paired learning.** This is the strategy that helped me do so well in calculus. My professor used a strategy called paired learning. Here is how it works. The teacher writes a problem on the board and walks us through it step by step. Then he has each of us make up a similar problem and swap it with a classmate. After we work the problem, we double-check our answers. If we don't get the same answers on both problems, then we talk about it and figure out the right one. The professor moves more slowly and makes certain that everybody understands before he moves on to a new concept.

➤ **Be a tutor.** I also tutored a friend of mine. In the process, I had to figure out the steps in order to explain the problems to her.

Katie's Advice:

➤ **Remembering math facts.** My mom and I made up a chart that has all my math facts on it. That way I can do my math problems faster.

Jeremy's Advice:

➤ **Use flash cards.** When I was younger and I was trying to memorize my math facts, I used flash cards to help me memorize my multiplication tables.

Perry's Advice:

➤ **Use a calculator.** If you still don't know basic math facts very well by the time you're in middle and high school, ask to use a calculator. It's written into my IEP that I can use a calculator in class and on tests. You can also have it included in your Section 504 Plan.

➤ **Get tutoring.** You might consider getting a tutor. I needed help in geometry and found it really helped me to have a tutor for that class.

I'll Do It Tomorrow

(procrastination)

You know you have an attention deficit if...

⇒ At 9:30 p.m. you remember that your semester chemistry project is due the next morning.

⇒ Crises caused by forgotten assignments are common. Your house looks like Office Depot because your parents keep a stockpile of poster board, magic markers, and report covers on hand.

⇒ You and your parents have stayed up many nights until midnight or later to finish a big project.

⇒ You put your homework off until the last minute.

⇒ Your favorite motto is, "Why do today what you can put off until tomorrow?"

⇒ You sometimes wonder, "Why can't I get started when I really want to?"

Fact: Experts tell us that many students with ADD or ADHD have great difficulty forcing themselves to start work on their chores and schoolwork. That may be why it seems like we can't get started until there is a crisis or pressure builds.  Typically, that means a major deadline has arrived; for example, a big project is due tomorrow morning. Finally the pressure jump-starts us and we begin working.

Because many students with attention deficits have major problems with important learning and organizational skills known as *executive function*, it really is more difficult for us to begin working, figure out how to do the work, finish the assignment, and then remember to turn it in to the teacher. It's not just a lack of will power.

Experts use these words to describe missing executive function skills that are essential for starting and finishing schoolwork; *activation, alertness, working memory, recall, processing speed, sense of time, internalization of language, reconstitution, and frustration tolerance.* Regardless of the technical words we use, the bottom line is that deficits in these executive function skills help explain why school is such a nightmare for so many of us who have attention deficits.

On the surface, putting homework off as long as possible makes us look like we're lazy or unmotivated or just don't care. But nothing could be further from the truth.

Because we know from experience that these reports and projects are so difficult, not surprisingly, we often put them off until the last minute. Executive function deficits are serious problems and teachers and parents must teach students how to overcome them. You can read more about executive function in Appendix 8.

Procrastination & Working under Pressure

I have a terrible time making myself do the more boring things in life that I need to do. Some may say I lack motivation, but it's really more complicated than that. *Until I get pressured,* I can't make myself work. The good news is that I've learned to work well under pressure. Later in life, you'll probably end up working well under pressure too. In fact, you'll probably do it better than most people because you've had lots of practice.

➤ **Getting started.** I always had problems getting started on homework, especially if it was something that was really hard for me like writing an essay. If I was interested in a topic and knew something about it, I could do the work pretty easily. In fact, I can still remember two of my favorite essays: "The Cursed Skull" (4th grade) and "The Last Flight of the Bird" (10th grade).

➤ **Starting on long-term projects.** When teachers gave me a long time to do a project, there was always something better to do, like riding my dirt bike or playing Nintendo. I figured I still had plenty of time. Next thing I knew the project was due. Sometimes I truly forgot, but other times I knew I had to do it. It's just that I knew it would be so-o-o hard and I hoped that if I put it off long enough it would eventually go away.

Advice on Getting Started

Alex's Advice:

Since problems getting started are part of ADD and ADHD, you may need to ask your parents, a teacher, or a friend for help. For example, they may need to remind you of your big projects and when it's time to get started on them. It's still really hard for me to make myself get started on projects I don't like to do. Here are some of the strategies that I used in high school and college.

> **Learn time management.** Your parents or teachers may be able to teach you time management—how to plan, prioritize, schedule and then do the work for the project. Time management is something that most people with ADD and ADHD have a terrible time doing right. There are some good ideas in Summaries 31-34 in *Teaching Teens with ADD and ADHD.*

> **Talk about the project.** Talk the project over with a friend or your parents. Discussing it may help you understand it better and develop a plan to finish it.

> **Read the directions.** Read over the directions with your parents and see if you can figure it out together.

> **Break the project into parts or segments so you don't feel overwhelmed.** Complete one part and then take a brief break. Then you can finish the next section and take another break. Or if it's a big project, spread the assignment out over several days.

> **Play a game with yourself.** If you have a reading assignment to do, tell yourself, "I'll read for fifteen minutes then I'll stop." Actually once you get started, you can read for a longer period of time.

> **Read to the clip.** Dr. Clare Jones, a veteran teacher and educational consultant, gives this wonderful suggestion: divide your reading assignment into three to five sections. Mark the sections with a colorful paper clip. Read to the clip and take a break. This strategy involves taking an "abstract concept"— reading a chapter—and making it concrete so that you can "see" when you're nearly finished. Otherwise, some teenagers will keep turning to the end of the chapter to see how much further they have to read.

> **Use physical activity to prime mental activity.** Try walking around while reading aloud from your book. Once you get started you can sit down and finish reading.

> **Consider a small dose of medicine.** If your medicine has worn off, talk with your doctor about taking a small dose to help you get through your homework.

Katie's Advice:

> **Take a break after school and then do homework.** I like to do my homework in the afternoon, but first, I take a break when I

get home. I eat a snack and maybe watch TV to clear my head. I don't need anybody to remind me to do my homework.

➤ **Be sure your meds are *still*/working.** After taking a short break, I do my homework while my medicine is still working.

Tyler's Advice:

➤ **Take a break first, then do homework.** Like Katie, I like to take a break when I get home, maybe an hour or so and then start on my homework.

Amelia's Advice:

➤ **Don't get any zeros.** Don't ever let yourself get a zero. Turn in something even if it's not up to your standards. Zeros averaged in with other grades are too hard to bring up to a passing grade.

Khris's Advice:

➤ **Set your Palm Pilot as a reminder.** I usually start working on my homework right after I eat dinner. I've programmed my Palm Pilot to remind me to get started.

Kati's Advice:

➤ **Pace yourself; break work into smaller parts.** Typically I have about three hours of homework to do over the weekend. It helps if I break it down into smaller segments. I work on it for a while and then take a break. Even though I have good intentions to do some work on Saturday, I usually end up putting it off until Sunday afternoon.

➤ **Give yourself a reward.** Sometimes I give myself a reward after I finish my homework. First I do my homework and then I can go to a movie with a friend or talk on the phone.

➤ **Ask your mom to remind you.** At times Mom reminds me when I need to get started on my homework. I usually like to do mine at night after dinner.

Adrian's Advice:

➤ **Do it now.** Don't leave things for tomorrow that you can do today.

Completing Semester Projects

I have to confess that at first I just thought I was lazy and that was why I put big projects off for as long as I could. Now I realize that it's more complicated than that. It always seemed like I started working on my major projects at the last minute. If I were lucky, I would finally remember and start working on it the night before it was due. This happened pretty often and really bugged my parents. Sometimes I had problems figuring out exactly what I was supposed to do. And even when I was ready to work, knowing how and where to start was also extremely hard.

Advice on Completing Semester Projects

Alex's Advice:

➤ **Ask for help.** I needed a reminder to get started early enough on big projects. Later on in college, I was finally able to do this on my own but it took me a while to learn to do that.

➤ **Keep extra supplies.** I forgot my projects so many times that my parents usually kept extra poster board and magic markers ready just in case.

➤ **Include notification of projects in your IEP or 504 Plan.** One student even had it included in his IEP that his parents would be notified when big projects were due.

➤ **Use a graphic organizer.** It may help you be more organized and feel less overwhelmed if you use a project graphic organizer like the one that my mom included in *Teaching Teens with ADD and ADHD*, Appendices A 5 and 6.

➤ **Ask the teacher about required projects.** Your parents could ask your teachers about long-term projects when they meet at the first parent-teacher meeting.

Amelia's Advice:

➤ **Write sticky notes.** I write myself sticky notes and put them in important places, such as on mirrors or in my sock drawer, to remind me when a long-term project is due.

Perry's Advice:

➤ **Start work immediately.** If a project takes a lot of time, I try to do at least half to three-quarters of it as soon as possible. I think that's a good work ethic and I try to make it a habit. I take at least fifteen to twenty minutes to look over the assignment, make some notes and start working on it. That way I have a plan and know if there is something that may take extra time.

Kati's Advice:

> **Use electronic sticky notes.** I've found that using these notes helps me remember all the details for semester projects. See NetNote at www.alshare.com.

Short Fuses

(difficulty controlling emotions)

You know you have an attention deficit if...

⇒ Your parents say you're so stubborn, you'd argue with a fence post.

⇒ You've been known to say, "I'm sorry I talked back to you, but I *am* right."

⇒ When you're really, really angry, you say whatever runs through your mind, even if it gets you in deep trouble.

⇒ Breaking up with a girlfriend or boyfriend feels like the end of the world. When that happens, you're so upset you can't seem to deal with anything else.

Fact: Experts tell us that it's harder for most teenagers with attention deficits to control their emotions than it is for other students. If you have ADHD, the problems are usually external or in other words, easier to see. For example, you may have a temper, get angry or frustrated easily and have a big blow up. You may even talk back, refuse to follow rules, or occasionally get into fights at school. Consequently, you may have yelling battles with your parents. These characteristics can also irritate your friends who, after a while may not want to spend time with you. Emotional issues such as breaking up with a girlfriend or boyfriend are earth shattering and may cause you to act impulsively and later regret your actions.

In contrast, those with ADD inattentive often struggle with issues internally—issues inside your head that may not be as easy to notice. You may be anxious, worry a lot, get discouraged easily, or feel bad about yourself. Unfortunately, a few teens will struggle with all of these issues. And then there are a few lucky ones like my friend Lewis who are always happy, never seem to get angry, and don't seem to have any problems with depression or anger.

When your levels of the neurotransmitter serotonin are high enough, you'll be happier and feel good about yourself. On the other hand when serotonin is too low you'll feel irritable, angry, argumentative, or maybe even aggressive.

Sometimes teenagers who are depressed may actually act aggressively instead of sad. In fact, some counselors believe that *aggression may mask depression.* In other words, when you're angry or aggressive, it may really be a sign that you're depressed. Stress and pressures at home and school can make your levels of serotonin drop. In addition, some people naturally have lower levels of serotonin.

A couple of things may help improve your life overall. Of course, exercise helps. Medication can also be very helpful. Doctors sometimes prescribe medicines like Zoloft or Prozac, because they help raise the levels of serotonin in your brain. These medicines help reduce conflict and make your life more pleasant. Sometimes if a student's aggression is causing major problems at home or school, doctors may also prescribe a medicine like Depakote, clonidine, or Lithium.

When you're passing all your classes, doing well in school and are happy at home, it's a lot easier to control your emotions. Experts tell us that the right medication can make your life a lot easier. You're more likely to succeed in school; get along better with your friends, parents and teachers; and feel happier.

Worry & Anxiety

I worry a lot although you would never know it just by looking at me. You would think I really didn't care much about anything. When I was in school, I constantly worried that I would say something stupid in class.

Advice on Reducing Worry & Anxiety

Alex's Advice:

➣ **Develop a plan.** Do something about what is worrying you. For example, if you're worried about failing math, get some tutoring. If you're worried about making a speech, then write an outline on the card or use overheads so you can't forget what to say.

- ➤ **Schedule "worry time."** Play a trick on yourself to limit your worry. Give yourself permission to worry fifteen minutes and then don't let yourself worry about it any more. During your fifteen-minute worry session, think, talk, and write about your worries, and don't let yourself do anything else for the entire time. Later, you can remind yourself that worry time is over.
- ➤ **Talk with your doctor.** Some students with ADD or ADHD may take a medication like Zoloft, Busbar, Prozac, or Celexa to treat their anxiety

Anger, Arguing & Talking Back

My parents and I never really argued very much. I was quiet and really didn't talk back to my parents. I might think some ugly thoughts about my parents or teachers, but I had enough self-control that I would not say them out loud. But my dad and my brother, who has ADHD, would have these terrible yelling arguments. They both could be pretty stubborn and loud.

Advice on Handling Anger

Alex's Advice:

- ➤ **Be alone.** When you're angry, go off by yourself until you can calm down.
- ➤ **Hit a punching bag.** If you have one, try hitting a punching bag. Sometimes screaming into a pillow will also relieve stress.
- ➤ **Go someplace calming.** Go sit in the woods or by a stream or swimming pool, or sit in your room and listen to music if that makes you feel better.
- ➤ **Get out of the house.** Go somewhere and do something so you can get your mind off your anger.
- ➤ **Brainstorm a solution.** Think of something to do to resolve whatever has made you so angry.
- ➤ **Check out the book,** *Teaching Teens*. In Summary 69 of that book, mom gives several more tips on anger management.

Kati's Advice:

- ➤ **Clear the air and apologize if necessary.** Unfortunately, it's hard for me to exercise self-control over what I say to my mother. Maybe that's because I'm worn out after I've worked so hard to keep myself under control at school all day. I think my mom understands how hard it is to have ADHD and she cuts me a little slack. She knows it's not personal. But there is a point where she draws the line. If we have a huge argument, I have to apologize to clear the air and get life back to normal.

Adrian's Advice:

➤ **Calm down.** I take a deep breath, think about the situation, and then go somewhere quiet and calm down so I can get back on track.

➤ **Let off steam in a good way.** You might even consider going to your room and screaming for a few minutes. That can help you get your emotions out.

Khris's Advice:

➤ **Stop and think.** It's important to stop and think if you find yourself getting angry. If I catch myself yelling, I try to remember to lower my voice. I also take some deep breaths and think about calming down.

➤ **Keep the peace.** Don't stay angry with anyone. Apologize even if it's not your fault. Keeping the peace is important.

Fighting or Blow-ups at School

Most of the time I was never in trouble at school. But one time when I was upset because I broke up with my girlfriend, I got into a fight with her new boyfriend and I was suspended. That was really a bummer.

Advice on Handling a Crisis

Alex's Advice:

➤ **Develop a crisis plan.** In case I ever felt like I was about to blow up at school, my mom, the guidance counselor and I developed a crisis plan so I knew what to do. When I was upset, I had permission to go talk to the guidance counselor. Unfortunately, when I went by the guidance office the morning before I had the fight, the counselor was out of the building at a meeting. Most of the time this plan worked; it was just a bad coincidence that the counselor was gone.

Anonymous Advice:

➣ **Use self-control.** The hardest situation for me to handle is if a teacher says something hateful to me. I get so upset inside. I have to exercise real self-control not to say something smart-alecky back. It used to hurt my feelings, but now it just makes me mad. I'm quick on my feet and often some brilliant comment pops into my head that would really smack them right in the face. But thanks to my medicine, I usually have time to stop and think about the consequences. "If I say this, will I find myself in front of the principal, get demerits, or end up having to go to Saturday detention?" In the end, I may still say something that I know will annoy them but not get me sent to the principal's office.

Kyle's Advice:

➣ **Walk away; refuse to fight.** I've learned to walk away from groups if I feel like I'm going to fight. I'm 5'10" tall and weight 190 pounds so I could fight if I wanted to. But I always refuse. I'll say, "Tell me why should I fight with you? What will that prove?" Then I won't talk to them; I just stare them down.

I really have to work to keep some of my feelings bottled up inside so that I don't say something I'll regret later. I can get so angry at times that I feel like I'm about to explode and curse out the world.

Nathan's Advice:

➣ **Ignore some people.** I ignore people when they make me angry. Sometimes I count to five and take some deep breaths.

Kati's Advice:

➣ **Walk away.** If I'm about to impulsively get into an argument or confrontation, I say, "Whatever!" and walk away. That works pretty well for me most of the time.

Breaking Up with a Girlfriend or Boyfriend

Even though you may have been thinking about breaking up with a girl, if she breaks up first, it may make you feel hurt and rejected. But when you stop and think about it, it's not really rejection. Dating different people *and* breaking up are a normal part of growing up. So the odds are great that you won't marry your first girl or boy friend. More than likely you'll date *and* break up with a lot of people before you become an adult and get married.

My parents always told me that there are "plenty of other fish in the sea," but you never want to hear them say that. At the time, I didn't understand their comment; in fact it irritated me. But now I agree; there really are other people to date. It will just take a while to find them.

Advice on Handling Hurt Feelings

Alex's Advice:

> **Take a second look.** Take the time to stop and look around when you're in a group. There are lots of other teens out there whom you can date; in fact, if you think back, there are usually a few who have given you a special look to let you know that they might be interested in you.

> **Stay busy; go out with friends.** Until you meet someone else, stay busy and go out with friends in a group.

Bouncing off the Walls

(restlessness; hyperactivity)

You know you have an attention deficit if...

⇒ You have trouble sitting still; you fidget, swing your foot, click your pen or doodle.
⇒ You've got to be on the go. You can't stand staying home. It's BO-O-O-RING!
⇒ You can't take "no" for an answer. When you want to do something, you keep asking and asking.
⇒ When you were little, you rode your Big Wheel down the basement steps.
⇒ As a kid playing cowboys and Indians, you had a noose around your neck, slipped while climbing a tree, and nearly hung yourself.
⇒ In kindergarten, you loved climbing up the bookcases.

Fact: Although teenagers with ADHD were hyperactive as children, their hyperactivity often disappears in adolescence when it seems to be replaced by restlessness. Luckily for you, the high energy often remains which means that you can keep going long after others are exhausted! Although teachers and parents may not like your high energy levels now, this can be good when you become an adult. Adults with ADHD can often work longer than others can. In fact, these adults may sometimes have two jobs at the same time.

Unlike teenagers with ADHD, students with ADD inattentive didn't have problems with hyperactivity when they were children. In fact if anything, they're under-active and sometimes may seem lethargic. Experts sometimes refer to this problem with under-activity, drowsiness, and lethargy as *sluggish cognitive tempo.* But in spite of their low energy, these teens still like to be on the go and are easily bored. "I'm bored" seems to be a common motto for most all teenagers with attention deficits.

One doctor who also has ADHD believes that some irritating and seemingly meaningless "ADD/ADHD behaviors," such as pencil or foot tapping, may actually serve a very important purpose. She thinks physical activity may actually *prime* mental activity. In other words, when you do something physical such as pencil tapping, it may help keep your brain more alert and make it easier for you to listen to adults and do your schoolwork. So use physical activity if it helps you stay alert. But be certain to pick something to fiddle with in class that doesn't make noise.

Restlessness

Teenagers with either ADD or ADHD seem to have problems with restlessness. Although I was never hyperactive, I do consider myself a restless person. I get bored easily, so I like to go places and do things. I hate staying home.

Advice on Restlessness

Adrian's Advice:

➤ **Avoid bad things.** When you're feeling bored, look for something to do that's not bad. When I was younger and got bored, sometimes I did things I regretted later. Now I'll go work on my low-rider bike for a while, draw, or go play pool with Pops.

Perry's Advice:

➤ **Take a walk.** When I feel restless, especially if I have work to do, I take fifteen minutes and go for a quick walk. Exercise definitely helps me get back on track. I try to do other things to avoid just sitting there. If I just stare into space, I really lose track of time and get even more distracted.

Kati's Advice:

➤ **Keep your hands occupied.** My brother, who also has ADHD, has to have something in his hands all of the time. If you can manipulate a pencil, pipe cleaner, eraser or squeegee while you're studying, it may help you stay focused and keep you from getting so restless.

➤ **Move your toes.** I actually move my toes inside my shoes.

Chapter 3

Coping with ADD & ADHD

There are several things that my parents and I did that helped me cope with all these challenges. I hope some of these strategies will be helpful to you and your family.

Major Issues

Here are my thoughts on several key issues, and some advice from our teen experts.

Education about ADD & ADHD

Educating myself about my ADD inattentive was more important to me than counseling. My parents spent a lot of time talking with me about my attention deficit. Most of the time they didn't talk very long—just a few comments about a particular problem I was having. They also showed me pictures of a brain and explained how neurotransmitters work. They told me about research in terms that I could understand. The more you know about attention deficits, the better off you are. You may want to read Appendix 5 to learn more about how the neurotransmitters in your brain work.

Advice on ADD/ADHD Education

Alex's Advice:

> **Learn all you can about your attention deficit.** It really helps when you understand how your ADD or ADHD affects your life. When you realize that so many of the things you do that bug your parents and teachers are related to your ADD or ADHD, then you don't feel like a bad person. Some of your questions may be answered in "Ten Frequently Asked Questions about ADD and ADHD" in Appendix 3.

> **Watch a video on attention deficits.** Mom produced a video of six of us talking about our attention deficits. We tell about

our school experiences and how medication worked for us. At times the video, *Teen to Teen: the ADD Experience*, is serious and at other times it's pretty funny. A lot of teens tell us they've enjoyed watching it.

➤ **Read a book.** In addition to this book, there are several others you may want to read: *Putting on the Brakes–Young People's Guide to Understanding ADHD* by Patricia Quinn; *Help4ADD@High School* by Kathleen Nadeau; *Making the Grade: An Adolescent's Struggle with ADD* by Roberta Parker; *ADHD—A Teenagers Guide* by James Crist; or *A Teenager's Guide to ADD* by Antony Amen, Sharon Johnson and Daniel Amen.

➤ **Ask your parents or someone else to tell you more about your attention deficit.** My parents gave me tips and taught me some skills to help me compensate for my ADD inattentive. So if your parents can't help you learn these things, then you should seriously think about going to your doctor, a teacher, or counselor who would be willing to help you learn more about your attention deficit.

➤ **Don't use your attention deficit as an excuse.** Of course, avoid using your attention deficit as an excuse. Instead, educate yourself and learn ways to compensate for its challenges.

Accepting Your ADD or ADHD

When you first find out you have an attention deficit, it can be kind of scary. What is this thing they're calling Attention Deficit Disorder? You may wonder what it really means. Is something wrong with me? At first you may deny you have it. You may say, "There's nothing wrong with me!" Or you may feel badly about yourself because school is so hard and you may think you're dumb.

Advice on Accepting Your ADD or ADHD

Amelia's Advice:

➤ **Don't let it get you down.** I first found out that I had ADHD in the sixth grade when I came home upset because I had failed a class at school. My disorganization was so bad that I did the homework, but would forget to turn it in to the teacher. At first I was really angry about having ADHD. I hated being dependent on medicine, hated having to take the medications, yet knew I really needed them so I could do well in school. I hated that I couldn't be a "normal" kid.

My advice is, "Don't let the ADHD get you down. If people make fun of you, don't listen. Believe in yourself!"

Erik's Advice:

➤ **Accept your differences.** I learn differently from others and I accept my differences. I usually ask for help when I need it and learn ways to help myself. However, I try hard not to let those differences stand out.

Succeeding in School

As I said earlier, we never did get my medication right in high school. Nor did we identify my learning problems or deficits in executive function, so high school was a nightmare. Despite the fact that I tried hard, I just barely got by. During most of my high school years, I was very unhappy and discouraged. It reached the point where I really didn't care if I passed or failed. Because being in school was such a negative experience, it wasn't something that I valued. Schoolwork was never exactly a top priority for me.

Homework was so difficult that I subconsciously avoided it. I was so disorganized that I often came home with papers stuffed in my notebook or backpack. Later, I would go through them with my mom. I had papers with no grades on them that I had forgotten to turn in to the teacher. Even though they said I was gifted, I had problems being organized and memorizing facts. It's a wonder I even graduated from high school.

Although I was always on the brink of failing, I think I only failed one class during my high school years. Luckily, my parents stayed on top of my schoolwork and I never got away with much. They would make me go back to school to get my books or call a friend for the assignments.

For me, school was more of a social time and the only reason I wanted to go was to see my friends. I really hated school and only went because I had to go.

When I went to college, I had to go back and review basic information, like grammar rules, that I had just scraped by learning in middle and high school. When I was in high school, I wasn't learning information—I was simply memorizing things. There is a big difference between memorizing and learning. Try to understand what you read instead of just memorizing information.

Life is better in school now for many students with ADD or ADHD. Teachers know more about the condition than they did ten years ago, and students are being diagnosed earlier. Medications are also better and they last a lot longer, so it's easier to pay attention all day at school.

Advice on Succeeding in School

Alex's Advice:

➤ **Don't just memorize; try to understand the material.** Some teenagers with attention deficits are not very interested in going to school and it's not something they like doing. If this is true for you, just remember, school is really hard for most people with ADD and ADHD. Roughly 50 percent of us also have learning disabilities, and that always makes school more difficult. I also know that we have to work harder than other students. In fact, I bet we have to try four times harder than other people. But the harder you work now the easier your life will be down the road.

➤ **Take these steps to be successful.** I found four action steps that are really important to be successful in school:
  ❶ get your medicine right
  ❷ identify your learning problems and accept accommodations such as untimed tests if you need them
  ❸ learn all you can about your ADD or ADHD
  ❹ learn to compensate for your problems
  These steps can make a tremendous difference in your life— once I got these things right, I didn't hate school anymore.

➤ **Check out my mother's book.** You and your parents may also find some helpful suggestions in *Teaching Teens with ADD and ADHD* that may help you do better in school. For example, my mom gives some suggestions on how to improve your memory and write better essays.

Accommodations at School

Looking back, I know the main reason school was so hard was that I didn't have the right medicine and dosage, and I didn't have any extra help for my disorganization and memory problems (executive function skills). Today students are eligible for special help known as *accommodations*. These are supports that teachers provide to help you succeed in school. Federal law requires that accommodations be given to students who have attention deficits that are serious enough to interfere with their ability to learn and do well in school. Typically, accommodations such as extra time on tests or using a computer make life easier for you. The teens who contributed to this book tell about the accommodations they're currently getting. By the time two of them were seniors, they found that they didn't need as much help.

Advice on Accommodations

Alex's Advice:

➤ **Accept help when you need it.** If you're in the same boat as I was, then you may need to let your parents and teachers help you more. Think of it this way; by letting others help you now, you'll learn the skills you need, and pretty soon, you won't need their help anymore. For example, I really needed extended time in high school and during my first couple of years in college, but during my last two years of college, I didn't need any accommodations except for one class. I started out the class without any help but realized I needed extended time for that one class. The last few years in college I made mostly A's. Learning is really important to me now.

➤ **Don't be too proud.** Most of us will need some accommodations at school, so don't be too proud to accept this help when you need it. Some students get beaten down by school failure and sometimes may want to quit. That's why extended time and testing in a quiet room by yourself are so important; they can help you be successful in school.

Medication

It's ironic, but teens with ADD or ADHD can't figure out what is going on with themselves and their attention deficit until they can concentrate. Obviously, if you can't concentrate on your problems and weaknesses, then you can't work on correcting them. You must get treatment and get the medicine right so you can concentrate on what you need to do!

When I was in high school, I really hated the fact that I had to take medicine. Life just didn't seem fair. At times I used to fight it and occasionally, would refuse to take it. But my parents and I would always talk it over and whatever I was worried about, they would try to fix. For example, I didn't want my friends to see me taking medicine at school, so I started taking an extended-release medication. Now I'm old enough to realize I really need to take my medicine so I can be organized and successful in life. Right now, I'm taking Adderall XR, which lasts ten hours. That works best for me. Of course, you'll need to talk with your doctor so you can find which medicine works best for you.

However, my brother was even more fortunate. By his senior year in college, he only needed to take medicine on the days he had Chemistry. Now, because he has a very active job, he doesn't have to take any medicine at all. Actually, back then he especially liked to take his medicine when he went deer hunting because he could sit in his deerstand longer.

Just so you know, when your medicine is working right, you'll see major changes in your life. You'll be able to pay attention better in class, make better grades, get along better with your parents and teachers, and feel better about yourself. If you don't see some positive changes, then chances are, your medicine is not working correctly. If this is true for you, talk to your parents and maybe even your doctor. You may be able to figure out what is wrong by reading more abut the specific things that medicine should do to help you both at home and school. Unfortunately medicine doesn't work at all for approximately ten percent of teens. Life can be extra tough for teens when medicine doesn't work.

Of course, medication is not a magic bullet. Although it helps a lot, it's not going to solve all your problems. You may still have some major challenges with disorganization, forgetfulness, difficulty memorizing facts, and time awareness problems, even when you're taking your medication. And of course, all your symptoms come back when your stimulant medication wears off. This means, you also have to do other things to cope with this challenge. For example, learn all you can about your attention deficit. The better you understand attention deficit disorder, the better you can cope with it. You'll have to work really hard to learn how to compensate for the challenges of having ADD or ADHD.

Advice on Medication

Alex's Advice:

➤ **If you're struggling, consider medication.** If you have been afraid to take medicine, don't be. Why not give it a try? If you don't like it or it doesn't work, then you can just stop taking it.

➤ **Become an expert on your ADD/ADHD medications.** I encourage you to take charge of your ADD or ADHD. One way to do that is to become an *expert* on your medicine. Do you know the name of the medication you're taking? Do you know how many milligrams you take? Do you know why it helps you pay attention? If you want to take charge and become an expert on your medication, then read Appendix 6.

➤ **Consider taking medicine when driving.** I really need to take my medicine when I drive my car. Experts like Dr. Russell Barkley, one of the world's leading researchers on ADHD, tell us that we can concentrate better and are safer drivers when we take medication.

Amelia's Advice:

➤ **Consider medicine.** I went through a period of rebelling against the medicine; I pretended to take it, but instead put it in my pocket. During the summers I sometimes refused to take it. Now that I'm older, I know I really need to take my Adderall XR. I always take it, especially when I drive and when I do my schoolwork. It helps me at work too, especially when I'm working the cash register. If I forget to take my medicine, the cash in my drawer never balances out right. But when I take my meds, I usually have a cash drawer that may be off by only a couple of pennies.

Erik's Advice:

➤ **Medication may keep you out of trouble.** I believe that being on medication (Concerta and Paxil) has saved me from myself on quite a few occasions, especially when my decisions would not have been thought through and I would have gotten into a lot of trouble. I've noticed that my life is more enjoyable when I'm on medication.

Khris's Advice:
➤ **Keep trying until you get the right medicine.** I've tried several medications and we can't seem to find the right medicine for me. We're still working with my doctor in hopes of finding the right one.

Tyler's Advice:
➤ **Different medications work better for different people.** Although Ritalin SR doesn't work very well for many students, I've found that it works best for me. When I'm on my  medicine, I'm perfectly focused and can get a lot of work done. Ritalin calms me down a lot.

➤ **A combination works best for me.** My doctor suggested that I take regular Ritalin and Ritalin SR (sustained-release) at the same time for the best results. When the two are combined, the medicine seems to last longer, maybe up to 5 hours, than just Ritalin SR alone.

Jeremy's Advice:
➤ **Don't be afraid to try medicine.** For a long time I wasn't open to taking medicine until I was forced to take it. I had some bad side effects that made me not want to take it. For example, at first it made me really tired and I wasn't as active on the playground. In addition, I wasn't as competitive in PE as I wanted to be and it affected my appetite. Now I'm happy that I did try medicine. I enjoy my life and feel so much better.

Kati's Advice:
➤ **Medicine helps at school.** I've found that my medications, Adderall XR and Welbutrin, really help me keep up with all my schoolwork.

Caution from the Authors: Neither my mother nor I am a doctor and we're not experts on medication. Obviously, we're not telling you that one medication is better than another and we're not endorsing any specific brand name medicines. Each teen is simply telling you which medication works best for him or her. The medicine that works best for me or one of the teen experts may not work well for you. Each of us responds differently to medication. In fact, medicine doesn't work for everyone. And even when medicine does work, it doesn't "cure" your attention deficit; it helps many of the symptoms get better for a period of four to twelve hours. So when the medicine wears off, the symptoms return. The most important thing you can do is educate yourself about medication and talk with your parents and doctor to decide what the best choice is for you.

Advice on Remembering Medication

Katie's Advice:

➤ **Set up a routine.** Having a routine helps me remember to take my medication. I keep my medicine in a daily dispenser and take it every morning when I come downstairs to eat breakfast. The medication dispenser is on the kitchen counter so I always see it and can remember to take it. The medicine takes an hour to kick in, so that way it's working by the time I start class.

Jeremy's Advice:

➤ **Use a weekly pill container.** One way I remember to take my medication is to put it in a weekly pill container and put it in the same place every day.

Side Effects of Medication

Most of us have experienced minor side effects from taking a stimulant medication. The two most common ones are listed first. A few other less common side effects are also listed:

❶ You may have trouble falling asleep if you take medication too late in the day.

❷ Medication affects your appetite and you may not be very hungry after you take your medicine. You may also lose some weight.

❸ In addition, some people also may have headaches or stomachaches that usually disappear after a while.

❹ Some teens may experience something called *rebound* that occurs as the medicine is wearing off in the late afternoon. During that time you may be irritable and your ADD or ADHD symptoms may be worse. These medicines may make a few people irritable but most teens seem to be more pleasant.

❺ You should monitor your growth, especially your height. Although researchers tell us that these medicines don't slow down our growth, it's best to be safe and talk with your doctor if you're not growing or gaining weight as you feel you should.

❻ Doctors tell us that if you also have bipolar disorder and take a stimulant medication as the first and only medicine, your symptoms may get worse.

❼ Some students who also have Tourette syndrome may find that the stimulant medications make tics worse. However, doctors who specialize in this area tell us that under careful supervision, most of these students can take stimulants without bad side effects.

❽ Experts also say that teenagers who may have heart disease, high blood pressure, or glaucoma should not take these medications.

Advice on Avoiding Side Effects

Alex's Advice:

➤ **Don't take medicine too late.** It's important to avoid taking medication too late in the day.

➤ **Eat before your meds kick in.** You should eat a good breakfast before you medicine has time to kick in and you may need nutritious snacks after school or later in the evening in addition to your regular evening meal. Sometimes you have to eat when you're hungry which may not always match up with the regular family meal times.

➤ **Talk with your doctor.**

  ➤ In situations where there is a history of substance abuse, your doctor may prescribe a medicine that is not considered as a risk for abuse like Strattera or Cylert.

  ➤ If bipolar is present, the doctor may prescribe another medication first, then recommend a stimulant later.

  ➤ Read more about bipolar and substance abuse in the section on "What if the attention disorder is not the only problem?"

Getting Medication Right

Getting the right medicine and dose is not easy and takes a lot of work. Trying to get your medication dose right is like going to the eye doctor for glasses. The doctor clicks the machine and says, "Tell me when your vision gets better." Then he flips to the next lens. If you say, "Yes that's better," then he may send you home without trying the next lens. You may be seeing a little better. You may even think you're seeing perfectly, when in fact you're not. You're still a long way from getting your prescription right. A few months down the road, you start thinking; this still is not the best it can possibly be. When you finally find the right medicine (medicinal perfection), it's like "Wow, this *really is* better."

We never did get my medicine right in high school. In fact, it has only been in the last few years that the medications have worked right. I really like the long-acting medications like Adderall XR and Concerta that last ten to twelve hours. These medicines give me a more normal day. Right now, Adderall XR seems to work the best for me. It helped me do the best in my college classes. Hopefully, you'll be luckier than I was and get your medicine right while you're still in middle or high school.

I always had an adjustment period when I started taking a new medication. It would take maybe a week for it to settle down and for my body to adjust to it. I noticed that sometimes a medicine helped me out the first day and then all of a sudden, it wasn't helping me anymore. I learned that it meant I was on too low a dose. Of course, the same thing may not be true for you, but if this happens to you, please talk with your doctor.

At other times the dose may be too high. Once when I switched from Ritalin to Dexedrine, I had a bad reaction. Later I found out that I was on too high a dose. Sometimes it's hard to know when medicine is too high because the milligrams in each medication are different. For example a five milligram tablet of Dexedrine is roughly equal to a ten milligram tablet of Ritalin. We didn't know that Dexedrine was more potent than Ritalin and switched over on an equal dose. I was really hyper and couldn't sleep for two days. It really scared both my mother and me. A year later, I tried Dexedrine again and it worked really well.

Advice on Getting Medication Right

Alex's Advice:

- **Ask yourself, "Is it working?"** Sometimes if the medicine is not working properly, it's hard to tell because you can't focus well enough to answer the question. So if someone asks you if your medication is working, and you find yourself saying, "I don't know," then more than likely it probably is not working very well.

- **Ask your teachers or parents.** Often teachers are the best ones that can tell if your medicine is working. Frequently your parents don't know because the medicine has worn off by the time you get home. Since you take medicine each morning, it should be working really well at school.

- **Use a medication rating form.** Here is a suggestion from my mother that may help you get your medicine right. If your teacher is not certain your medicine is helping, maybe you should ask her to fill out a medicine rating form such as the one in Appendix 7. Then you can take the results to your doctor. That will give you a better idea if the medication is right at school.

- **If needed, try the same medicine again.** Remember, just because you try a medicine once and it doesn't seem to work right, don't give up on it. The initial medication dose may have been too low or too high. If you're struggling and can't find a medicine that works, it may help to try the same medicine again later, so discuss this with your doctor.

- **Work with your doctor.** You may need to work with your doctor until you get the medication right. This could take a while, so be patient.

When Treatment Is Not Right

It's a sad statement to have to make but when medication is

not right and you don't have any accommodations for your learning problems, school becomes a punishment. I compare ADD/ADHD school struggles to a runner who has sprained an ankle, yet is trying to participate in the Olympics. You're still on your first lap, and the other athletes are already on their last one. Then the next thing you know, all of the other runners are finished. Everyone in the stadium is watching you. Do you really want folks to watch you hobble off the track? You're so embarrassed that you just quit the race after your first lap,

I reached the point after so many failures at school that I would get halfway done and then just quit working. I felt like why even bother to start. If you continue to fail in school, then after a while you just give up. Even when I was a senior in college, most students in my classes were "test sprinters." At best, I was a "speed walker."

The experts say that *multimodal treatment* is the best strategy for helping us cope with our attention deficits. That means that you should use a variety of strategies like taking medicine, educating yourself about your attention deficit, getting help for your learning problems at school, and participating in counseling to learn new strategies. It also includes parent training, ADHD education, and counseling for your parents.

Advice on Getting Treatment Right

Alex's Advice:

➤ **Play detective.** Sometimes when life is not going well at home and school, you need to play detective and figure out what the problems are. Then develop a plan to correct them. Frequently three or four major problems may keep treatment from going well:

➤ Your medicine is not right.

➤ You have learning problems, but don't have any accommodations at school.

➤ You have some problems with organization and memory that are caused by deficits in executive function.

➤ You have a coexisting problem such as anxiety or depression that is not being treated.

➤ **Seek multimodal treatment.** As I just explained, the experts recommend a broad approach to treatment not just medication and counseling. That means that you should use a variety of strategies:

➢ Get educated about your ADD or ADHD, how it affects you, and strategies for coping with it like those given in this book. For example, you may read a book, watch a video, or attend a teen panel to see what other teens have to say about having attention deficit disorder.

➢ Talk with your doctor about medication.

➢ Work with your teachers to get any accommodations you may need to address your learning problems or executive function deficits. You or your parents may be able to suggest learning strategies that are most effective for you. For example some of the tips listed in *Teaching Teens with ADD and ADHD* include giving visual cues and using hands-on activities.

➢ Get treatment for any coexisting conditions like anxiety or depression.

   ➤ For example, experts tell us that counseling can be effective in teaching strategies for coping with your anxiety.

   ➤ "Talk therapy", or just talking about your problems, may not be as helpful as learning new skills and strategies, a process known as "skills training." The experts tell us that there is no proof that skills training works for younger children. However, I think we're older, more mature and capable of learning from "skills training" classes. For example, these classes could address issues like:

     → Organizational and study skills

     → Test taking skills

     → Anger management

     → Money management

     → Conflict resolution

     → Social skills

     → Self monitoring; rating your own work at school to prompt yourself to keep working

     → Using "self-talk" to help make good choices; ("Stop and think." Or "Is that a good choice or a bad choice?")

    Of course, the hardest thing will be finding someone who teaches these classes in your local community.

➢ It's also critical for your parents to help you find an activity that you do well and develop that skill such as

> programming computers, working on cars, or participating
> in sports or religious activities. You need to find an activity
> that you love doing and you're really good at.

> ➤ It may be helpful to get a tutor or an ADHD coach. Or your
> parents may have to act as your coach for a while until you
> get your academics under control. Drs. Edward Hallowell
> and John Ratey tell about the importance of coaching in
> their book, *Driven to Distraction.*

> ➤ Hopefully your parents will also attend parent training
> classes plus counseling if needed.

Making & Keeping Friends

Sometimes teenagers with attention deficits have trouble making and keeping friends. Unfortunately, experts tell us that 50 percent of children with ADHD have problems with relationships with their friends. Perhaps it's because if you're not on your medicine, you may be more likely to be loud, aggressive, bossy, or interrupt others. Any of these behaviors may be annoying to your friends or classmates and they may not want to be around you. If you have ADD inattentive you probably get along with your friends pretty well because you don't tend to act the same way as students with ADHD. Typically you're usually quieter and a little more laid back.

Have you noticed how we can always spot someone else who also has an attention deficit? As a result, in high school most of my friends had an attention deficit too and they all hung out at my house. Two nice things about hanging out with friends who also have attention deficits are our forgetfulness and inattention. If someone says something stupid or insults us, we forget it pretty quickly or we may not even notice we've been insulted.

Advice on Making & Keeping Friends

Alex's Advice:

> ➤ **Medication is a huge help.** Whether you have ADD or ADHD, it's
> easier to get along with friends when you remember to take
> your medicine. When you're on your medicine, you're less likely
> to say something you'll regret later. You're also less bossy and
> less likely to get angry and blow-up.

Kati's Advice:

➤ **Listen hard and ask questions.** Sometimes I get a little anxious when I meet new people. But when I do meet people, I work hard to listen to them, be interested in what they say, and ask questions. I really like people and would never be mean to anyone. Occasionally I may say something hurtful without thinking. But all of my friends like to joke with each other, so it usually works out okay. Some of my friends see me as different, but I think it's okay to be unique! I have no problems being me.

Adrian's Advice:

➤ **Pick good friends.** Look for good friends that won't force you to do things that you don't really want to do. When I was younger, I finally realized that some people weren't good friends because they kept getting me in trouble.

Jeremy's Advice:

➤ **Be yourself.** When my ADHD was diagnosed in kindergarten, it was a big shock for me. I felt like I was really different from everyone else. Middle school was the hardest for me. I had an identity crisis; I was afraid to just be me. I tried really hard to fit in by changing myself. I guess I figured that other people might not like me because I was so different

At times it seemed like some people couldn't handle my ADHD. I talked a hundred miles an hour and my thoughts came just as fast. Sometimes I came up with ideas so quickly that people didn't understand them and couldn't keep up. So I began to feel like a loser. I became depressed and that's not a good place for any of us to be. As a result, I separated myself from other students; I was afraid to get close to people. The teenage years are hard even if you don't have ADHD. With the changes in our hormones during puberty, our feelings are really complicated and they pull us in many different directions.

But the good news is that I made it through middle school and my identity crisis okay. Later, when I attended a larger high school, it was easier to find more people like me. So don't set yourself apart from the crowd just because you have an attention deficit. Get out of the box and find the people you can fit in with. The main thing is to just be yourself!

Accepting Help from Others

The books for adults with ADD or ADHD by Dr. Hallowell and others talk about the importance of finding an ADHD coach to help you do the things you're not very good at such as being better organized, planning for the future, or managing your money. You don't have to be a genius to figure out that if adults need a coach, teenagers definitely need one, maybe even two. Unfortunately, ADHD coaches who work with children and teens are rare. So in reality, your parents or a good friend often become your ADHD Coach. Or you may be lucky and find a good counselor or tutor who can help you.

One of the hardest things for me to do was to accept help from my parents, but they made me a deal. They said that as long as I was passing my classes, they would not check to make certain I was doing my homework. But in classes like algebra that I was always on the verge of failing, they usually checked my homework every night. They also checked to see which classes had major projects due. I was notorious for forgetting big projects until the night before they were due. This always put the whole family in an uproar.

Hopefully, we've convinced you that it really is okay to accept help! Think about this—when we're learning how to play baseball, basketball, or hockey, learning to scuba dive, or driving for the first time, someone has to teach us these skills. Sometimes we learn on our own by trial and error, but for the tough stuff, we need help. According to Dr. Ted Mandelkorn, a pediatrician, "It's ironic that school is the only place where we give the message that you should not need help." Clearly, when we're struggling with disorganization and forgetfulness caused by an executive function deficit, we need help!

Advice on Accepting Help

Alex's Advice:
> ➢ **Accept help when you need it.** The bottom line is that you're

probably going to need help. Let those around you help so that you'll pass all of your classes. Life is so much easier when you're doing okay in school. You won't need this much help all of your life. Later on you'll learn new skills that will help you compensate for your attention deficit.

➤ **Include key issues in your IEP.** If it's a major problem for you to remember your big projects, ask that it be addressed in your IEP or 504 Plan. That way you and your parents will be given advanced notice when a major project is due.

Amelia's Advice:

➤ **Tutors can help.** The only way I passed Algebra II my senior year was that I went for tutoring after school with my algebra teacher three days a week. She was amazing.

Erik's Advice:

➤ **Accept help from your parents.** I'm fortunate enough to have my parents support in all of my scholastic endeavors even though it's annoying at times. But I have to give credit where credit is due. My mom e-mails my teachers frequently and she holds me accountable for my work.

➤ **Attend a study skills class.** My one regret is that I didn't have a study skills class until I was in the tenth grade. With direct instruction, I had someone telling me to get my work done and holding me accountable. That year, my grades were the best I had ever gotten. I maintained at least a 3.0 all three trimesters. I really could have used it in the ninth grade because I was constantly overwhelmed with homework. The stress and failures I endured in the first two trimesters in ninth grade put me into severe depression.

➤ **Use weekly reports.** My IEP says I'm supposed to get weekly progress reports so I can see where I am all the time. This holds me accountable for my work.

Ari's Advice:

➤ **Accept a tutor.** I have a great tutor right now who is a big help to me. Occasionally, she talks to my teachers to clarify some of my assignments. Of course, she asks my permission first before she talks with them.

Nathan's Advice:

➤ **Use note cards.** I have a hard time studying by myself, so my mom and I review my notes everyday and put key points on note cards. Then I keep my notes cards and review them before a test.

Tyler's Advice:

> **A tutor can help with writing essays.** I have a tutor who has been teaching me how to write better essays.

Kati's Advice:

> **Find a good tutor who is also fun.** My tutor understands ADHD and tries to make learning fun for me.

Counseling

In some ways my situation was unique because my mother was a teacher, school psychologist, and a counselor. So for better or worse, I had my own personal teacher and counselor all my life. Here are some of my thoughts about counseling.

I can think of three types of counselors I've had—my pediatrician, psychologists, and psychiatrists. I really liked talking to my pediatrician best and going to the Pediatric Center was nice because everyone has to go to the doctor. I didn't feel like I was bad or that something was wrong with me. Somehow, it didn't even seem like I was going to a counselor. Plus I didn't have to sit there and talk to someone for a whole hour.

I could tell my pediatrician really liked me, understood my attention deficit and just accepted me for the way I was. He helped me feel good about myself. He helped my parents too because they didn't know very much about attention deficit disorder and were really worried about how it would affect me.

I know that some teens have found counseling helpful, but most of the time I hated having to go. One time when I went to a counselor, she was negative and kind of on my case. None of us liked her so I never went back. I got a new counselor.

I think it's hard for most counselors to relate to teens and it's hard for us to talk to someone we hardly know and to accept advice from them. It takes a long time to learn to trust someone. I guess that's why I liked having my mom for my counselor.

I also went to psychiatrists at times to get my medicine right. I liked some of them but not others. The best ones really listened and didn't judge me. It takes a special person to get down on a teenager's level. If they can't do that, they won't be effective counselors.

Just because somebody has been to school and received a degree doesn't mean that they know what they're doing. I found some doctors who thought they understood ADD and ADHD, but they really didn't have a clue.

Maybe one reason that counseling wasn't always very much help is because I also had good common sense. I could figure things out. I rarely ever had a psychiatrist tell me something that I didn't already know. Of course that's exactly what some experts say, "People with ADHD know what to do, but don't always do what they know."

Erik's thoughts on counseling: No teenager wants to admit they have a problem or that their parents think they have a problem. I think most kids are afraid to ask for help. It's like admitting we have a weakness. It takes a lot of courage to ask for help. I know that from experience.

I had a really bad year when I was in the ninth grade and went to see a counselor. I was only 14 and didn't get a lot from it. Most of the time I blew it off because I didn't want to be there. It seemed to help my parents the most. My counselor did help me in one way; he pointed out things I didn't recognize. For example, I was feeling pretty stupid at school, and he reminded me that I *was* smart.

Kati's thoughts about counseling: Overall I think counseling is beneficial. However, one of the disadvantages of counseling is that you have to wait too long for an appointment. By the time my mom and I could get an appointment with the counselor, we had already worked out our problems. One of the reasons I didn't like going to the psychiatrist was because we would bring up my problems. Sometimes I really didn't want to be reminded about them.

Advice on Counseling

Alex's Advice:

> **Find someone you trust.** Even if you don't want to go, counseling may be a good idea especially if you can learn just one new thing that helps you. My best advice is to find someone you

like and trust and work with them. It's important that they treat you with respect and not make you feel badly about yourself. In my opinion, the person who has down-to-earth practical experience will be far more helpful to you in dealing with your ADD or ADHD.

Erik's Advice:

➤ **Look around for a good counselor.** Everyone's experience with a counselor will be different. It will be best if your parents shop around and check out the counselor first. You should talk to someone you like and trust.

➤ **Get your parents to go for counseling.** My parents used what they learned in the counseling sessions to help me at home.

➤ **Others can also help.** It's really easy to talk with my pediatrician because he also has ADHD. We have a good connection because he understands and can relate to my problems. My sixth grade teacher also helped me build friendships. She understood my ADHD and went out of her way to help me.

Kati's Advice:

➤ **Talk to your pediatrician.** My pediatrician was the best counselor for me. He is very down-to-earth and was always willing to talk with me if I needed help. I like it better when we talk one on one, not with my parents there. I like when my doctor explains my brain to me. For example, he tells me when I do something impulsive that I'm not getting enough dopamine and serotonin in my prefrontal cortex. He also has helped me get along better with my brother.

Parent Counseling

One of the neat things my parents did was to go to counseling for themselves so they would know the best way to work with me. Of course, at the time I didn't know that's what they were doing.

Advice on Counseling for Your Parents

Alex's Advice:

➤ **Encourage your parents to learn all they can about attention deficit disorders.** My parents always said that counselors come and go, but parents stay forever.

➤ **ADD/ADHD education.** It's really important that your parents learn everything they can about ADD or ADHD and how to help you succeed in school, in other words "ADD/ADHD education."

➤ **Skills training.** Your parents should also benefit from counseling sessions aimed at teaching them better parenting skills such as communication skills and conflict resolution techniques.

➤ **ADD/ADHD education for you.** Your parents also need to make certain that you're educated about your ADD or ADHD. When you learn something new from this book, tell your parents about it. That way, they may learn some new information too.

Getting to Know Your Teachers

During the teenage years, it's pretty natural for some tension to exist between teachers and students. When I was in high school, I refused to do anything that might look like I was "brown-nosing" teachers. Sometimes I didn't even know my teachers' names.

Advice on Relating to Teachers

Alex's Advice:

➤ **Get to know your teachers.** If you're smart, you'll work to get along with your teachers. I just decided that I would come home later and clean off my brown nose. It's important to get to know your teachers. You want them to know that even though you're struggling, you're really trying hard.

➤ **Teach your teacher about attention deficits.** Educating teachers so they understand ADD and ADHD is also very important. Visit www.chadd.org for some fact sheets that you can give to your teachers. Information from this book may also be helpful to teachers. In addition, Mom has some good basic handouts for teachers in her books, including "What Every Teacher Must Know about ADD and ADHD" in Summary 1, *Teaching Teens with ADD and ADHD.*

What If the Attention Disorder Is Not the Only Problem?

According to a landmark study by the National Institute of Mental Health (NIMH), two thirds of the students with ADHD also had at least one other condition. The same neurotransmitters that cause our symptoms of ADD or ADHD may also be involved in causing some of these other problems. Here are some of the other coexisting conditions that you might be struggling with:

Anxiety

Approximately one third of teens with ADD or ADHD are also very anxious. When you have anxiety, you may be afraid of making a mistake, worry a lot or bite your fingernails. Extreme anxiety may involve a panic attack that includes a pounding heart, difficulty breathing, dizziness, trembling, nausea, or fear of going crazy. You may be especially anxious in class, because you know you don't always pay attention, so you worry about being called on in class and not hearing the question or not knowing the answer. You also worry about misplacing your homework and forgetting an upcoming test.

Obsessive-compulsive disorder

A form of anxiety in which you may have the same thoughts over and over or have to do the same things again and again. For example, you may have to wash your hands over and over again or check and recheck math problems that you have done, even though you know they're right.

Depression

Roughly one fourth of teenagers with ADD or ADHD are also depressed. Typically, if you're depressed you may be in a bad mood a lot, don't enjoy life, or are irritable or aggressive. There may be several reasons why you're depressed: school is so hard, it seems like you can't do anything right or adults are on your case all the time.

Learning disabilities

One fourth to one half of all students with attention disorders also have learning disabilities. You may have trouble writing essays, memorizing facts, such as multiplication tables, spelling words, history dates, or understanding and remembering what you read.

Tourette syndrome

Roughly ten percent of teens with ADD or ADHD also have Tourette which means they may involuntarily repeat certain sounds and actions over and over. In other words you can't control the fact that you may constantly clear your throat, blink your eyes, shrug your shoulders, or lick your lips. You may find more helpful information on this topic in the book, *Teaching the Tiger* by Pruitt and Dornbush.

Sleep problems

As we explained earlier in the book, approximately half of all teens with attention disorders have problems falling asleep or waking up.

Aspergers

Although Aspergers doesn't occur that frequently, it's a very challenging condition. If you have Aspergers, you have trouble recognizing and responding correctly to the emotions of others; so you seem to lack empathy. In other words, you may laugh at something that everyone else thinks is totally inappropriate, such as when someone is badly hurt. You may always look either angry or unhappy and find it very hard to make and keep friends.

Bipolar disorder

Eleven to twelve percent of teens with ADD or ADHD also have bipolar disorder. Because some of the symptoms of ADHD and bipolar are so much alike, it's very hard to tell these two conditions apart. When you have bipolar, you may have mood swings that go from one extreme to another—from being depressed to being hyper and irritable. As a little kid, you may have been extremely irritable; thrown huge tantrums that last a long, long time; talked a lot as fast as you could; had major sleep problems including bloody horrible nightmares; been aggressive and destroyed things. Occasionally, a few people also experience hallucinations or delusions, like thinking they can fly.

Oppositional behavior

Roughly two thirds of students with attention disorders are oppositional. Typically that means you may lose your temper easily, argue with adults, talk back, or refuse to mind your parents or teachers. Sometimes a teen may received an official diagnosis of *Oppositional Defiant Disorder.*

Substance abuse

The two most commonly used substances among teens with ADD or ADHD are cigarettes (50 percent) and alcohol (40 percent). Marijuana is third at (17 percent). Obviously, substance abuse can be a major problem for some teens with attention deficits. So the best advice is: "Don't ever get started!"

The most serious substance abuse problems often occur in people with an attention deficit and either conduct disorder or bipolar. If you have been diagnosed with either bipolar or conduct disorder, then you're at risk for having serious problems if you chose to use drugs. So the best advice is don't do drugs. Be very careful and avoid situations where you're exposed to drugs.

If you have only ADHD and not conduct disorder and ADHD, you're no more likely than your friends to end up with a serious substance abuse problem. In fact, according to the experts, if you take medication to treat your attention deficit, you're *less likely* to abuse drugs than others who have untreated ADD or ADHD. Read more on substance abuse in the next section on "Tough Topics."

Conduct disorder or law breaking behavior

Roughly twenty percent of teens with the most serious problems are said to have a conduct disorder. That means you have taken advantage of the rights of others, or have broken the law by stealing, destroying property, being cruel to people or animals, fighting or using a weapon. If someone says you have a conduct disorder, then chances are good that you also have several other conditions that are making life hard for you. For example, experts tell us that people with conduct disorder have an average of four other conditions such as depression, anxiety, bipolar, or substance abuse. So if these conditions are treated, you're likely to feel much better and not get into as much trouble.

Advice on Coexisting Conditions

Alex's Advice:

> **For more information.** If you're curious about any of these coexisting conditions and want to read more, you can find additional information in *Teaching Teens with ADD and ADHD*

and *Teenagers with ADD and ADHD.*
➤ **Seek treatment.** When you have any of these conditions, you may act in ways that really make your parents angry. They may think you're just being ornery, or lazy or are a bad person. For example, when you're depressed, you may be irritable, get angry easily, not have the energy to do your schoolwork, and want to sleep a lot. All of these conditions will get better when they're treated. Talk with your doctor or ask your parents to talk with him or her to determine if any extra help is needed.

Finding Your Special Talents

Since school was such a nightmare, one important thing that my parents did was to help me find activities that I did well. Doctors Bob Brooks and Sam Goldstein called this finding my "islands of competence." We looked for areas outside of school where I could be successful. Some of the things we tried worked out really well, such as learning to use a computer, working on electronic gadgets, taking swimming and scuba diving lessons, and learning to water ski.

Advice on Finding Your Special Talents

Alex's Advice:
➤ **Find your "Islands of Competence."** You and your parents need to find activities that you really enjoy, and then practice so you can become really good at them. For example, I've known people with ADD and ADHD who were really good swimmers, baseball players, school debaters, saxophone players, fishermen, car mechanics and dirt bike riders.

Advocating for Yourself

It's very important for you to learn to advocate for yourself. Learn as much as you can about your ADD or ADHD, then you can make your teachers aware of how you learn best and your specific learning challenges. You'll also know what accommodations you need and can make certain that you get them in middle school, high school and college.

Advice on Advocating for Yourself

Alex's Advice:

➤ **Take charge of your life.** Ask teachers for the supports you need to succeed at school. Make certain that you get the accommodations that are included in our IEP or 504 Plan. For example, if the teacher forgets, you may need to remind him or her that you need a quiet room when you take a test. Ask your parents for help or talk with them about what you need to get your homework done. You may want to work at a desk, listen to a radio, or begin homework at seven o'clock every night. Or you may ask your mother to type an essay on the computer as you dictate it. If you and your parents are arguing about schoolwork, talk to them and work out a compromise. For example, if they nag you about getting started on your homework, suggest an alternative like setting a timer to remind you to start working at seven o'clock.

Katie's Advice:

➤ **Help develop your IEP.** At my last IEP meeting I told them that I didn't need any accommodations right now. But when I need any help, I'll ask for it. It's really important for teenagers to be involved in developing their IEPs and telling adults what they need and which accommodations will work for them. They also need to say what doesn't work because many teachers may try common modifications that are not helpful to some students.

Erik's Advice:

➤ **Participate in your IEP.** I'm always very active in my IEP meetings and tell my teachers what I need. Having a good IEP is absolutely necessary for me. Because of the supports provided through my IEP, I'm becoming more self-sufficient. I don't need as much help now.

Tough Topics

There are some issues I need to bring up that are hard to talk about, but they're important and need special attention. I really feel like these things need to be said.

Medication or Illegal Drugs?
Which One Will It Be for You?

For some teenagers, coping with ADD or ADHD eventually comes down to a choice between medication and illegal drugs, including alcohol and cigarettes. Unfortunately, a couple of my friends with attention deficits had serious problems with drugs. I think they were *self-medicating*—in other words, they were taking illegal drugs to relieve the symptoms and stress of having an attention deficit disorder. The bad news is that they ended up getting addicted to drugs and ruining their lives rather than making them better.

During high school, my friends and I were always feeling stressed. Most of us didn't think we were doing a good enough job at home or school. It seemed like we were always down on ourselves. I think we were trying to get away from feelings of incompetence and just wanted to feel better about ourselves.

Some people do drugs to help them reach a level of relaxation. For a short period of time they can be free of all stress. Taking illegal drugs helps people escape but it really doesn't solve their problems.

I found that medicine makes you productive, so you don't need those other drugs. Medication addresses problems and helps you do the things you have previously avoided. Medicine helps you out; it doesn't just help you escape.

Two doctors named Tim Wilens and Russell Barkley did some very interesting research. In separate studies, they both found that people with ADHD who took medication were *less likely* to abuse drugs than people with ADHD who didn't take medicine! Think about what that means; if you take medicine now when you need it, you may be less likely to abuse drugs later in life.

The same thing is true if you just have ADD or ADHD without a co-existing condition—you're not as likely to abuse drugs either. However, if you have a an attention deficit along with several other problems, such as failing at school, a really bad relationship with your family, plus another condition like conduct disorder or bipolar, you run a greater risk of getting hooked on illegal drugs. Like I told you earlier, if you have an attention deficit and one of these two co-existing conditions, then it's so important to stay away from drugs. Don't ever get started.

Advice on Making Good Choices

Alex's Advice:

> **Medicine or illegal drugs? You decide.** For me, taking medication is a smarter solution to our problems. The decision to do drugs or take medication is like being at a major fork in the road; one path leads downhill to a lot of trouble and the other leads uphill to a better life. Remember, taking medicine as prescribed is legal; we don't have to worry about hiding it or getting into trouble for taking it. It has helped me become a better person.

> **Figure out what you need to do to succeed in school.** The other thing you have to do is figure out how to succeed in school. Work with your parents and teachers to figure out why school is so tough and ask for accommodations to help you. Experts also tell us that students who do well in school are less likely to abuse drugs.

Advice on Using Drugs while Taking Medication

Alex's Advice:

> **Don't do it.** It's not smart to use any other drugs like alcohol, marijuana or cocaine when you're taking your medication. Each drug you add has a certain toxicity level or poisonous effect that could have an extremely bad reaction with the others. A drug like cocaine can actually stop your heart from beating.

Smoking & Attention Deficits

Experts tell us that cigarettes are the substance most frequently used by teenagers with attention deficits. Nearly fifty percent of us will end up smoking. Like my grandfather, I started smoking when I was twelve years old. I knew it was really bad for my health so I quit smoking when I was in college.

Smoking is really disgusting in a lot of ways—it makes your breath smell bad and your clothes, room and car all stink. If you have friends who don't smoke, they hate the way cigarettes smell. Sports are harder because you get out of breath easily. And you may accidentally burn holes in your clothes or damage furniture

I used to smoke when I was uptight about school and life in general. Later I realized that smoking was just another way of self-medicating. The nicotine in cigarettes seemed to calm me down and that helped me pay attention a little better. I also felt more alert. But there are healthier ways of paying attention. Nicotine is very addictive and once you start smoking, it's one of the hardest habits to break.

Advice on Smoking

Alex's Advice:

> **Don't ever start smoking.** The best advice I can give is simply to never start smoking. If I could go back and do it over again, I never would have started because it's so-o-o hard to stop. Don't let your friends talk you into smoking because before long, cigarettes control your life and you can't quit, even when you want to. My grandmother has emphysema now because she smoked for years. She has to use oxygen all of the time and it's really scary when she can hardly breathe. If you take the medicine your doctor prescribes for your attention deficit, hopefully, you'll never get hooked on smoking.

Driving & Attention Deficits

Well I'm probably the last person in the world who should be giving advice on driving because this has been one of my biggest challenges. Hopefully, if I warn you about the problems I had, you'll be able to avoid them.

First let me give you some facts. Dr. Barkley tells us that teenagers with attention deficits are four times more likely than their friends to get speeding tickets and have wrecks. Our friends tend to learn their lessons when they get a ticket and have an accident, but we don't. We're seven times more likely than our friends to have a second accident and most of the time it's our fault.

Some of the characteristics of our attention deficits play a role in our problems driving, like being impulsive, not paying attention, always being late, trying to make up time, and hyperfocusing on one part of driving but not paying attention to our speed. So as you can guess, your parents are going to be very nervous when you start driving. A lot of states have passed some pretty tough driving laws, so that if a teenager gets even one ticket, it's possible to lose his or her license for a long tme. It's a good idea to work out some plans with your parents to keep you driving safely.

Advice on Driving

Alex's Advice:

➤ **Take driving lessons.** One important thing you can do is to take driver's education.

➤ **Practice driving with an adult.** You should spend several hours practicing with one of your parents or another adult in the car. Some states require fifty hours.

➤ **Develop rules with your parents.** Some teenagers also develop rules with their parents and sign a driving contract. My mom has an example of a contract in *Teenagers with ADD and ADHD.* Some parents give graduated privileges. That means you start out driving during the day in good weather and progress to driving at night, and then even in bad weather. And be sure to wear your seat belt.

➤ **Consider medication when you drive.** My parents always said, "You have a choice; if you want to drive, then you must take your medicine." Otherwise I didn't pay attention while I was driving.

➤ **Don't carry passengers at first.** When you first start driving, experts recommend that you not have any passengers in the car with you. Extra teens in the car increase the chances of having a wreck.

Amelia's Advice:

➤ **Consider medicine.** I always take my medicine when I'm driving.

Closing on a Note of Hope!

When I was younger I always enjoyed computers. But, it was more of a hobby for me and I never saw myself as being any better at it than anybody else...at least not until I decided to minor[2] in computer science in college.

Suddenly I found myself doing better than most of the people in my classes, as in, staying within the top three students in all my computer classes. But that was just the beginning. Strangely enough, other students started asking me for help on projects and assignments. Not only that, but the entire time I was taking classes in the computer department, not once did I meet another person who was only getting a minor in computer science. That's right; the people who were asking for my help were all majoring in software engineering, network administration, and business information systems.

The real kicker came when one of my professors told the class something that I knew didn't work because I had tried it before. I didn't want to contradict him in class, so I stopped by his office later and told him how I had gotten it to work. The next day he told the class how to do it right. For the rest of the semester, any time he would say something that he was unsure about he would glance at me for confirmation before completing his sentence.

In another one of my classes, the professor had been offering an extra credit project for several semesters. No one could complete it because they couldn't figure out how to write one part of the program. This section was actually the first part of the assignment that I was able to program.

So, sometimes it helps to have an attention deficit because you may think about solving a problem in a way that most people would never even think about. Now that I've graduated from college, I'm doing some part-time computer consulting, web page design and network installations earning a very nice salary.

My point is that you should not get down on yourself because you

---

[2] Students in college select their major course of study and declare a "major"; a second area is called their "minor". Typically a student who minors in a subject doesn't take as many courses and is not as knowledgeable as students who major in that subject.

feel like you don't have anything worthwhile that you can do well. You do have something special; it just might take you ten years to realize what it is and just how well you can do it.

The reason I know you have some special skills is simple. When something is interesting, you not only learn it but you get so absorbed in it that you end up learning more about it than the average person would. And you can't tell me you don't get absorbed in the things you really like, because that's what's happening when you're playing a video game and you don't hear your mom or dad loudly calling your name from two feet away.

The good news is that ADD and ADHD are being diagnosed earlier these days. We're getting better treatment earlier. The new medicines are lasting longer and working better. As a result, more of us are avoiding the terrible experiences of failing in school.

Let's be honest though; life still won't be easy for us. In other words, having an attention deficit is really, really hard, but don't let yourself get discouraged when things are not going your way. One thing that helped me make it through school was to think about Albert Einstein. He did terribly in school and teachers didn't like him. Yet he still turned out to be one of the greatest geniuses of all times.

When I was a kid growing up, I only knew about Einstein but later I learned that other famous people, including geniuses such as Edison and Disney, had failed many times before ultimately becoming successful.

Because we have an attention deficit, occasionally we're going to make mistakes or even get into trouble. But we have to think of these situations as an opportunity to learn from our mistakes. We can overcome the challenges of having an attention deficit! So let me leave you with this thought for when you're feeling overwhelmed and discouraged:

"Mistakes are a natural part of life. We learn by experimenting; mistakes and failure can be important parts of our learning process. Einstein flunked grade-school mathematics. Edison tried over 9,000 kinds of filaments before he found one that would work in a light bulb. Walt Disney went bankrupt five times before he built Disneyland. If we accept our setbacks, we can continue to risk, learn and move on with excitement and satisfaction."

(A quote from a California Department of Education task force included in *Raising Resilient Children* by Robert Brooks, Ph.D., and Sam Goldstein, Ph.D.)

Appendices

Appendices:

More Helpful Information
for You & Your Parents

A Letter to Parents of Teenagers with ADD or ADHD

Appendix 1: Interview with Alex at Age 16

Appendix 2: How Do I Know If I Have ADD or ADHD?

Appendix 3: Ten Frequently Asked Questions about ADD & ADHD

Appendix 4: The ADD/ADHD Iceberg

Appendix 5: What Do I Need to Know about My Brain?

Appendix 6: What Do I Need to Know about Medication?

Appendix 7: A Medication Rating Scale

Appendix 8: Executive Function: "What is this anyway?"

Appendix 9: A Graphic Organizer for Writing an Essay

Appendix 10: The ADD and ADHD Dictionary

A Letter to Parents of Teens with ADD or ADHD

Dear Parents,

Alex and I have written this book for you in the hopes that it will help you understand what it's like for a teenager to live with ADD or ADHD. Despite some terrible struggles in school and against the odds, my son, Alex, graduated from college recently. I'm extremely proud of him, his accomplishments, and his courage and tenacity to stick with and finish college. As you can tell from reading this book, however, our lives didn't always look so rosy. During the teenage years, we were frightened about what the future held in store for him. Since our lives are much happier and more optimistic now, we wanted to share the lessons we've learned with other families. Here are some of the things we learned.

ADD and ADHD are very common—lots of young people have it. In fact there are probably up to 2-3 million (5-12 percent) children and teenagers under the age of 18 with an attention deficit living in the United States. So now you know…you and your teen are not alone! Many children and teenagers just like yours are trying to figure out how to live with the challenges of having an attention deficit.

As you already know, there are many difficulties that go along with having ADD or ADHD. School is probably the biggest challenge for most teenagers. For example, students with attention deficits may forget their homework assignments, get lots of zeros on homework, have trouble remembering what teachers or parents tell them to do, struggle to memorize multiplication tables, be late to class or dinner, or lose things that are important. When teens have these problems, some parents and teachers who don't know any better may fuss at them for "not trying hard enough." Some adults may even say to the teenager, "You're lazy" or "You don't care. Of course these statements are not true, but they still make teens feel badly about themselves. As a result, many students with ADD and ADHD really hate school. Attention deficits left untreated may eventually result in a student dropping out of school.

The good news is that there are some steps that you, your teen and teachers can take right now to make life easier. Two federal laws, *IDEA* and *Section 504,* offer important help. For example, teachers can help teenagers by giving them special supports known as *accommodations.* These accommodations help teens compensate for the learning problems that go along with having ADD or ADHD. When students with attention deficits are asked which classroom accommodations are the most helpful, they often say getting *extended time* on tests or essays.

Another effective strategy that helps students succeed in school is to *take a medication* like Ritalin, Adderall, or Concerta. Most students can concentrate better and get more work done at school when they take medicine. As a result, experts tell us that students make better grades and behave better at school. This makes teachers and parents happier and they're less likely to be on the teen's case. Most of the time when teenagers get extra help, they can be successful and happy in school.

There is hope for the future! Sometimes we say that people with ADD or ADHD are "late bloomers," which means they take a little longer to mature and grow up than their friends. So when your teenager grows up, life will probably be easier for him or her.

➤ First of all *they will know more about ADD and ADHD* and how it affects their life.

➤ Second, *they'll learn how to compensate,* or learn tricks that help make up for the challenges of having this condition. For example, if they have trouble being on time, a special watch, beeper, or Palm Pilot can help remind them of the time. They could also ask someone, perhaps a friend or later on a secretary, to help them remember.

➤ Third, *attitudes about behavior change,* especially when teens get out of school. For example, some teachers are irritated by children who are hyperactive, talk a lot, or who disrupt class by making people laugh. However, in the grown-up work world, these people are often well-liked, make other people laugh, and have tons of energy.

  ➤ One young man, who was the hyperactive class clown, has found the perfect job. He is doing on-air advertising promotions for special events at the local radio station. With his high energy (hyperactivity) he can work long hours. In fact for a while he had to work three jobs until he could get full-time work at the station. He once worked as a manager for a company that installed lawn sprinkler systems— another great job for him. He liked working outdoors and could talk as much as he wanted.

➤ A girl who was hyperactive grew up to do a very exciting, challenging job; she is a firefighter. Other jobs that people with attention deficits may like are an emergency medical technician or a salesman.

➤ There are a lot of jobs in which having ADD or ADHD doesn't cause major problems. For example, we've known people with attention deficits who were electricians, policemen, managers of manufacturing plants, college professors, doctors, photographers, veterinarians, and computer programmers.

➤ Last but not least, hopefully *they will find someone who is good at the things they have trouble doing well*—for example a friend, parents, or a spouse who can help them remember homework assignments or when they're older, remember to pay bills.

To help teenagers prepare for their future and career, there are a few important steps you can take now:

➤ **Educate your teen.** If your teen is to feel in control of his or her life, he or she must learn everything possible about this condition and how to treat it.

➤ *Help your teen learn everything he or she can about ADD and ADHD.* Reading this book should help. However, let's be realistic. Chances are good that your teen may not want to read this or any other book. So you may have to read one section, possibly highlight key points, hand it to your teen, and say nothing or say something like, "What do you think about this?" Or leave the book lying around in obvious places complete with highlighting and bookmarks in key sections. Hopefully, curiosity will get the best of your teen and he or she will read portions of the book.

➤ Depending on your teen's interest, you might even *read* about a specific topic *together.* If possible, read the whole book together over a period of time; don't just wait for a crisis.

It's probably not best to ask your teen to read this information when you're in the middle of a heated power struggle with him or her. You may need to wait a day or two after you've had problems with an issue. For example, you may read about anger and then ask a few questions like: "Does this sound like you? or Do you see any advice on this page that you think might work for you? Why don't we try it this week and see if it works."

➤ Remember to *listen* to your teen's answers. It's critical to involve your teenager as a respected partner. You're working with them to help them cope with this very challenging condition. Through this process you're empowering your teenager to take charge of his or her attention deficit, and you're also teaching the skills needed to accomplish this goal.

➤ *Use this book as a springboard for discussion.* My goal for this book was to provide a neutral springboard for discussion that helps remove the direct conflict between parents and teens regarding specific problem areas. For example, in discussing sleep problems, you can talk about the facts rather than criticize the teen for "being lazy." You might say, "A lot of teens with attention deficits have problems falling asleep and getting up. Here are some suggestions for resolving these problems. Do you think any of these might work for you?"

➤ Watching the video *Teen to Teen: The ADD Experience,* may also be helpful. It's available from www.chrisdendy.com and www.chadd.org.

➤ *Review the DSM-IV criteria* for attention deficits (Appendix 2). Sometimes we assume that teenagers know what an attention deficit is, when in reality they may have no clue as to why the doctor has diagnosed them with having ADD or ADHD. You may want to read through the criteria together and ask which one they think they have, ADD, ADHD, or ADHD combined.

➤ *Teach your teen about his medicine.* Teenagers need to know the name of their medicine, the dosage and how frequently they should take it. They should also understand how long it lasts and what changes to expect in their school performance and behavior. Otherwise, they won't know whether it's working properly.

➤ **Ensure success at school.** One of your most important jobs is to ensure academic success for your teenager. Teachers can't do this important work alone; a parent-teacher partnership is essential. Work with teachers to identify learning problems and provide needed accommodations. *Teaching Teens with ADD and ADHD,* my second book is devoted to helping ensure that your teen is successful in school. You'll learn about important intervention strategies to address common challenges such as writing essays, memorizing information, math, IEPs, Section 504 plans, functional behavioral assessments, behavioral intervention plans, and much more.

➤ **Develop new skills.** Encourage your teen to not be afraid to learn new skills, even if they're not very good at them. Fear of additional failure may make teens afraid to try new experiences.

➤ **Teach your teen to compensate.** Teach your child to compensate for his or her ADD/ADHD-related problems. The advice given by the teens in this book is a good place to start.

➤ **Identify and develop talents.** Figure out what your teen's special talents are and give him or her opportunities to develop them.

 ➤ Encourage participation in activities like art classes or a computer camp that he or she enjoys.

➤ **Keep your teen's future career in mind.** Think ahead about a career because most of our teens will not. Identify a few career ideas that might work for them and help them develop skills that may be needed in that type job. For example, Alex was really good with computers, so I signed him up for computer classes. He took every electronic gadget in the house apart, rarely putting anything back together. In the process he learned a tremendous amount about electronics. Two potential career paths evolved for him: computers and electronics.

 The activities teens love now may eventually be the keys to a future career. Active jobs that require hands-on work are usually better suited for these teens than a job that requires them to sit at a desk eight hours a day. Doing paperwork all day sounds too much like doing homework so you can probably imagine how they would feel about that!

➤ **Don't be afraid to help your teen plan for the future.** For example, you may have to fill out the application for college or a job, ask the teen to sign it and then mail it. He or she will get better at planning ahead but just remember, developmentally your 18-year-old is more like a 12-year-old. Not many 12-year-olds are capable of submitting a college application without help.

➤ **Teach driving skills.** Help your teen safely master driving skills. We want teenagers to live long enough to enjoy happy, productive lives. I give several tips about teen driving in my first book, *Teenagers with ADD and ADHD.* For example, I talk about the use of logical consequences, dealing with insurance and tickets, and going to court. In addition, when Alex graduated from high school, they came out with a computer monitor that you can put in a car (www.driveright.cc). One of my colleagues, Dr. Marlene Snyder, has written a more detailed book that you might find helpful, *ADHD and Driving: A Guide for Parents of Teens with AD/HD.* (www.whitefishconsultants.com)

A few final words of advice:

➤ **Become an ADD/ADHD expert.** Learn everything you can about ADD or ADHD, medications, common learning problems linked to attention deficits, and what to ask for in the way of help from schools. Attend local advocacy meetings such as those offered through CHADD or ADDA-SR. Local CHADD chapters are listed at www.chadd.org. The Attention Deficit Disorder Association-Southern Region lists its local chapters at www.adda-sr.org. You also should consider a parenting class where you can learn effective strategies. I offer several helpful parenting strategies in *Teenagers with ADD and ADHD* and *Teaching Teens with ADD and ADHD.* Here are two of my favorites:

   ➤ *Give choices.* When you give teens a couple of choices, they're more likely to comply with your requests, finish their schoolwork and be less aggressive. Here is an example: "Do you want to start your homework at 7:00 or 7:30?"

   ➤ *Use depersonalization.* You might say something like this: "Students with attention deficits have trouble remembering their homework assignments. I've noticed this is a problem for you at times. What kind of system can we work out so you don't forget your assignments?"

➤ If you have a daughter, you will want to learn more about the unique challenges caused by hormonal changes, societal expectations, and biological differences facing girls by reading Patricia Quinn and Kathleen Nadeau's books on girls and women: *Understanding Girls with AD/HD, Understanding Women with AD/HD,* and *Gender Issues and AD/HD.* Sari Solden is another well-known author who addresses women's issues.

➤ **Tell your teen it's okay to accept help from others!** In fact while they're still in school, it's very important to let others teach them tips for coping with their attention deficit. The main reason they need help is because they have a four to six year developmental delay which means they mature at a later age than their friends. Later on, when they learn these tricks, they will be able to handle almost every challenge by themselves.

➤ **Get your own personal fears under control.** Obviously, there will be times when you'll be very frightened. You may ask yourself, "What does the future hold? What if my child doesn't make it?" I know because I've been there too. I was especially vulnerable at each new developmental stage. After Alex graduated from high school, I worried—"What if he can't graduate from college?" I seemed to be picking some point, years in the future to worry about.

Remember, fear is palpable; it's like mist in the air. You can't see it very well, but you can definitely feel it. If you're frightened, your teen will sense it, so keeping your fears under control is critical. Give yourself pep talks on a regular basis. Making encouraging statements helps too. At times I would say to Alex, "Honey, I know things are really tough for you, but just remember, you and I are going to make it through this." If you feel you can't control your anxiety, especially if it's interfering with your relationship with your teenager, then talk with a counselor or your doctor about the best way to cope with it. You may benefit from counseling or taking medication for a brief period of time.

➤ **Don't take things personally.** You'd better develop a thick skin and be prepared to be frustrated or have your feelings hurt. Frequently, parents are on the receiving end of their teen's angry, frustrated feelings. You're the safest person they know; you love them and will never give up on them. So you may become their target. Hopefully, as you implement an effective multimodal treatment program, most of their major problems will get better.

➤ **Don't give up hope.** Just in case your teenager can't seem to get his or her life together after high school, don't give up hope. Dr. Mark Katz tells us about research from Hawaii on *resilience* in youth that explains how many young adults take advantage of a second chance at success. For example, joining the military, getting married, having a child or having a significant relationship may give the young adult the strength, energy, and inspiration to get back on track in his life. The most important thing your teenagers have going for them is knowing that you as their parents still believe in them and will be there to help out when needed.

I trust you'll agree that Alex has done a terrific job of explaining ADD and ADHD from his perspective. We both hope that this book will help you and your family cope successfully with your teen's attention deficit. Best of luck to you and your family as you grow together through the incredibly challenging teenage years.

Warm regards,

Chris Abney Zeigler Dendy

Appendix 1: _____

Interview with Alex at Age 16

"When you have a disability like ADD or ADHD, you don't know what "normal" attention and concentration are. You just assume that everyone concentrates the same way you do. It's like having a vision problem. You don't know what the real world looks like or that you have a vision problem until you're tested and get glasses. You don't know you can't see until you put on glasses the first time and realize that trees are not just big blobs — they're made up of individual limbs and leaves. In the same way, you don't know you have ADD/ADHD and problems with attention and concentration until you take Ritalin4 and find out what it's like to be able to concentrate.

"Second grade is where the trouble started. This is where I discovered writing, and that I didn't like it. One day when I was frustrated, I stopped writing. When the teacher asked me to do the work, I mumbled under my breath and told her to do it herself.

"In third grade I didn't get along with my teacher at all. She couldn't understand why I was so slow, so I spent a lot of time with the principal. This teacher was so bad that even my parents didn't like her.

"I wasn't doing well in school and they referred me to be tested. I scored pretty high and they said I was eligible for the gifted program.

"In fourth and fifth grade I was lucky enough to get the same teacher. Having the same teacher helped me with my work habits. The thing I liked best about this class was its pets, especially the snakes. I liked taming wild snakes, and I was bitten almost every day.

"I wasn't prepared for sixth grade. It was exactly like high school. I had six classes, six teachers, and six homework assignments everyday. This was a big change for me, but I hung in there.

"In seventh grade I moved to Georgia from Florida. The schools became a little bit less like high school since I only had three teachers instead of six. Unfortunately, I got myself into trouble by cursing at a teacher. This incident helped me in a way, because I became good

---

[3] Published in *Teenagers with ADD* in 1995.

[4] Back when I started taking medication, Ritalin was the main prescription taken for ADD. It would only last 3-4 hours. Now I take Adderall XR and it lasts 8-12 hours.

friends with the principal.

"In eighth grade I was transferred to another school. Mr. Ford, the principal, also transferred to the new school. That year one of my teachers wasn't a friendly teacher, but I controlled my temper this time.

"Ninth grade wasn't as bad as I thought it would be. Some of the work was harder for me, which caused me to slack off a little bit. Actually, I was failing four of six classes at mid-term. But my parents stayed on my case and checked all my homework in the classes I was failing. I was so glad when I started passing everything so my they didn't check my work so closely. The Ritalin also helped me a lot when I was trying to do my homework.

"My sophomore year seemed to be a little bit easier, but I still slacked off some. I would usually have low grades that I would pull up near the end of the semester. My grades were pretty much borderline, but I had a few high grades.

"So far my junior year has been the same with borderline grades. "Sometimes I was a troublemaker at school. I didn't like to do the work. Sometimes I made fun of the teacher. Teachers said I didn't assert myself very much. My parents said that teachers told them that I was never a discipline problem. I guess the things I did to make them mad were pretty subtle. I didn't do anything real bad. Mainly I just thought bad things about a few of the teachers.

"I like for my teachers to treat me with respect. If a teacher is nice to me, then I usually do better in that class. If I don't like them and I think they're mean, sometimes I'll fail the class.

"When I'm not on Ritalin, I tend to be more impulsive and more aggressive. I go on instinct. When I'm on my medicine, I actually think about my decisions more clearly and what will happen if I do something. I can do my work better when I'm on my medicine. I can really concentrate a lot better. I can sit for two or three hours and work on my homework.

"I'm not constantly on Ritalin so I can't constantly think about what will happen. Unfortunately, I forget why I was grounded and feel like my parents are just being mean to me. It doesn't connect in my mind that I really did something wrong. Punishment doesn't work a lot of times because it doesn't connect in my mind.

"I've been stopped for speeding lots of times. I hate to tell you, but I was stopped for speeding several times during the first year I was driving. Lately, I've slowed down a lot. Now, tickets and speeding are starting to connect in my mind a little more. I have to go to court and

pay money. They take my license away. But once you get your license back and are out driving, you forget. You don't realize that they can take it away again. I always say I won't do this again after I get a ticket. Getting a ticket really upsets me and I feel really stressed out. My Toyota 4-Runner is the love of my life. I live to drive.

"If you asked me to describe myself; I would say I try to be generous to other people. I get along well with a lot of people. I have a lot of friends. My friends say I'm a take-charge kind of guy. I'm adventuresome. I like to come up with ideas. I try to make things fun."

Appendix 2: _____

How Do I Know If
I Have ADD or ADHD?

Let me briefly explain how doctors decide if you have an attention deficit. Here are some basic facts you should know:

➤ **There is no single test that confirms that you have attention deficit disorder.** The doctor looks at a lot of information and has to make a judgment about whether or not you have ADD or ADHD.

➤ **Underachievement or doing badly in school is usually a key symptom.** Teachers may fill out a checklist that shows where you have problems. Report cards may contain comments like "does not pay attention," "fails to complete work," and "does not use time wisely." Teachers may say, "You're really smart but you are not living up to your potential."

➤ **In order to be given an official diagnosis of ADD or ADHD, you must be having problems in two places.** In other words, it usually shows up both at home and at school and later on at work.

➤ **The official list of symptoms of ADD and ADHD is contained in a document called the DSM-IV.**

Diagnostic and Statistical Manual, fourth edition (DSM-IV)
Here is a simplified list of the symptoms:

1) Inattentive. Doctors call this **ADHD, predominately inattentive**; teachers call this **ADD.** You will be diagnosed with this type of attention deficit if you have six of the nine symptoms listed below.

    ⓐ Doesn't pay close attention to details or makes careless errors
    ⓑ Difficulty sustaining attention
    ⓒ Doesn't seem to listen

    d Doesn't finish chores or schoolwork
    e Disorganized
    f Avoids schoolwork and homework
    g Loses things
    h Easily distracted
    i Forgetful

2) Hyperactive-Impulsive. Doctors call this **ADHD, predominately hyperactive-impulsive**; teachers call this just plain **ADHD**. These symptoms describe what you were like in elementary school. You will be diagnosed with this type of attention deficit if you have six of the nine symptoms listed below.

  Hyperactivity
    a Fidgets or squirms in your seat
    b Can't stay in your seat
    c Runs or climbs a lot (teenagers may feel restless)
    d Difficulty playing quietly
    e "On the go;" acts if "driven by a motor"
    f Talks a lot
  Impulsivity
    g Blurts out answers
    h Can't wait for your turn
    i Interrupts; butts into conversations or games

3) Combined hyperactive and inattentive. If you have a total of 12 symptoms, six in each section, then doctors say you have ADHD Combined Type. Teachers also call this ADHD.

If you want to know more about diagnosing ADD or ADHD, several good books are listed in the References & Resources list. The official diagnostic criteria for AD/HD are contained in the Diagnostic and Statistical Manual, Fourth Edition (DSM-IV). Washington, DC. American Psychiatric Association, 1994.

Appendix 3: _____

Ten Frequently Asked Questions about ADD & ADHD

Here are answers to ten basic questions teenagers often ask:

1. What is ADHD? What is ADD?
ADHD stands for Attention Deficit Hyperactivity Disorder and ADD stands for Attention Deficit Disorder. Often, the term ADHD is used broadly to include all students with an attention deficit, even those who are not hyperactive. A lot of people use these words interchangeably, in other words to mean the same thing.

Actually, experts in different fields have different names for attention deficit disorders. In the education field, teachers use the terms ADD and ADHD. However in the medical field, doctors call *all* attention disorders Attention Deficit/Hyperactivity Disorder, even if you're not hyperactive. Doctors list three different types of the condition:
➤ AD/HD predominately hyperactive and impulsive
➤ AD/HD combined type
➤ AD/HD predominately inattentive

AD/HD inattentive is the same thing that teachers call ADD.

We use the terms ADD and ADHD in this book because they are logical and make better sense to the average person.

2. What is the difference between ADD and ADHD?
The simple answer is that people with ADHD are hyperactive and those with ADD inattentive are not. Students with ADHD have trouble paying attention, do or say things impulsively, and were hyperactive as children. By the teenage years, the hyperactivity is often replaced by restlessness. In addition, teenagers with ADHD usually have high energy and like to talk a lot. On the other hand, students with ADD inattentive tend to be a little quieter and more laid back. Typically, they do things more slowly and don't have as much energy as teens with ADHD. Teenagers with ADD are also restless and have trouble paying

attention, but for slightly different reasons.

3. How many people have ADD or ADHD?

Experts tell us that 5-12 percent of all children and teenagers have an attention deficit disorder. That means in a class of thirty students, there will be a least two or three teenagers with ADD or ADHD. In the United States, there are probably between 2-3 million youth who have been diagnosed with this condition.

4. How many boys versus girls have an attention deficit disorder?

Boys are diagnosed with attention deficits more often than girls. In fact, for every three or four boys who are identified, only one girl is diagnosed. Some experts like Drs. Quinn and Nadeau argue that girls have attention deficits just as often as boys. These experts think that the symptoms of attention deficits in girls are slightly different from those in boys. Consequently, girls with ADHD may often be overlooked because they're not as hyperactive or aggressive as boys with ADHD.

5. Why do I have trouble paying attention?

One simple way of explaining this is to say that your brain works differently from students who don't have ADD or ADHD. This is not a bad thing, but it does make paying attention in school really tough. Experts know that if you *could* pay attention, you would! Rest assured that inattention is not caused by laziness!

To be honest, experts are not exactly certain why students with ADD and ADHD can't pay attention easily. Their best guess, however, is that *chemical messengers* of the brain, known as *neurotransmitters,* don't work exactly right. When this happens, students have the symptoms of ADHD such as inattention, impulsivity, and hyperactivity. Scientists think that the neurotransmitters called *dopamine, norepinephrine and serotonin* may be involved. This process is described in more detail in Appendix 5.

Let me explain why it's so difficult for teenagers to pay attention to schoolwork that's not very interesting or fun to them. When most students listen to a teacher, they pay attention for a few seconds, look away, move around in their seats, and then *redirect* or bring their attention back to the teacher. Once students with attention deficits shift their attention away from routine and possibly boring schoolwork, it's very hard for them to shift it back. Many adults don't realize that you must constantly struggle to bring your attention back to your schoolwork.

Unfortunately, teens with attention deficits quickly grow tired of reading boring material and begin looking for something more interesting. From a biochemical perspective, *your brain requires that activities be stimulating* in order for you to stay alert, pay attention and continue to do your schoolwork. When schoolwork is boring or routine, you often have difficulty with a lack of *persistence of effort*—trouble sticking with your work. As a result, teachers will often complain of uneven academic performance—one day you can do your schoolwork and the next day you can't.

6. Why is school so hard for me?

The characteristics of ADD and ADHD—inattention, impulsivity, and occasionally hyperactivity—make it very hard for students to pay attention, concentrate, and complete schoolwork on time.

Most students with ADD and ADHD struggle at school—experts tell us around 90 percent. There are several good reasons why school is so hard.

> Students with ADHD may also have *learning disabilities.* The Centers for Disease Control and Prevention (CDC) reported that approximately half of all students with ADD or ADHD have learning disabilities.
>> Twenty-five percent of all students with ADHD may have a learning disability in *math.* For some students that means they have a terrible time learning multiplication tables. Even though students may practice and practice, they still may have trouble remembering these facts.
>> Sixty-five percent have problems with *written expression,* so writing essays or answering essay questions on tests is very difficult for them.
>> Other students, roughly thirty percent, have trouble with *spelling.*
> Some students also have serious problems with organization, memory, and planning skills known as *executive function.* This means that many students have trouble remembering homework assignments, planning ahead to complete a long-term semester project, or planning for the future. Problems in this area have been one of the major reasons that teens with attention deficits have such a terrible time in school.

Unfortunately, many adults think these problems are just due to laziness. They don't realize that these problems are related to executive function deficits. Therefore, it's critical for parents to learn all about executive function and how to help teens compensate for any problems in this area. For more information read Appendix 8. And for additional coping strategies, refer to *Teaching Teens with ADD and ADHD,* Chapter 3.

7. Is ADD or ADHD the same for everyone?

Students with ADD or ADHD are not all alike. For example, a student may have symptoms of ADHD that are mild, moderate, or severe. In addition, some students with ADHD are hyperactive and others with ADD inattentive are not. Students with ADD inattentive tend to have less energy and may process things more slowly. But in high school, most of these teenagers seem to be restless instead of hyperactive. These students get bored easily, want to be on the go, and can't stand to stay at home.

In addition, researchers at NIMH found that two thirds of these students have at least one additional condition that makes school even harder. For example, some students may also be depressed, anxious, or have learning disabilities. As a result, they may worry a lot, bite their fingernails, cry, get angry easily, argue a lot, or talk back. Sometimes, even when they try very hard, they still can't do well in school.

Unfortunately, when students have a complex case of ADD or ADHD that's not being treated properly, they may feel so overwhelmed that they experiment with illegal substances like cigarettes or marijuana. Some experts think they may actually be *self-medicating,* in other words, using illegal substances because it makes them feel better. To learn more about self-medicating read "Medication or Illegal Drugs" in Chapter 3, Coping with ADD and ADHD.

There are several hidden or less well known characteristics that often show up in students with attention deficits, such as, sleep problems and having no sense of time. Some of these are addressed in the ADD/ADHD Iceberg in Appendix 4.

8. What causes ADD and ADHD?

ADHD is inherited, which means it runs in families. Over half of the students with ADHD also have at least one parent with it. In addition, about one third of students with ADHD have a sister or brother with the same diagnosis.

First, you have to remember what you know about how neurotransmitters work in the brain. Simply stated, the chemicals in the brain don't work exactly like they should. Experts have also found differences in the brain's structure. Here is what they have learned:

> Researchers have identified several *genes* in the brain that they believe are linked to attention deficits.

> There is *reduced blood flow* in important parts of the brain. The reduced absorption of glucose, the body's fuel, means that the brain is underactive.

> The brain's *white matter is slightly smaller* in certain areas. The white matter contains the connections between the neurons and these connections carry messages from one neuron to the next. Scientists, however, didn't find any brain damage; the white matter was simply smaller.

You will find more information on the brain and medication in Summaries 5 and 6.

Children inherit certain genes in the brain that control how the chemical messages are sent from neuron to neuron. When neurotransmitters work right, students can pay attention. Currently, experts believe there are at least thirteen genes involved in attention deficits. Here are the names of the ones they think are the most important: *dopamine receptor genes* known as DRD2 and DRD4, and a *dopamine transporter gene* known as DAT1.

In other situations, a person may have a bad accident or events may happen during pregnancy that can also cause an attention deficit. For example, if a pregnant mother abuses alcohol, drugs, or cigarettes, the baby may be born with ADD or ADHD.

9. Does medication help?

We know from research that medication helps most children and teenagers, between 75-90 percent of all students. When medicine is right, great things can happen. Students can pay attention better, work harder and get better grades in school. They also get along better with their parents and teachers. You may want to read more about medication in Appendix 6.

Of course medication is not going to make everything perfect but it's the best treatment intervention we have right now. Sometimes it may not work exactly right the first time you take it. If the initial medication doesn't work after careful fine-tuning, it's very important to try another one.

Here is a somewhat simplified explanation of how medicine works. Pictures of the brain taken with a PET scan (positron emission tomography) show underactivity or reduced blood flow in certain areas involved in doing schoolwork. When adults took a stimulant medicine, the PET scan showed increased or normal blood flow and the adults did better on certain tests. The medication enables the neurotransmitters to work better, resulting in greater activity and increased blood flow in the brain. This means that you can pay attention better.

Some teenagers may be afraid to take their medicine for fear that they might become addicted to drugs. However, researchers have found that when students with an attention deficit take medicine, they're *less likely to abuse drugs* later than those with ADHD who don't take the proper medication.

If for some reason, you can't take medicine, we don't want to scare you. You can work with your parents and other adults to do everything else listed in "Getting Treatment Right" to make it unlikely that you will be tempted by illegal drugs. Being successful in school is critical!

Some teenagers don't need to take any medication once they get out of high school or college. However, other teens with more complicated cases of ADD or ADHD may need to take it for most of their lives.

10. Do you outgrow ADD or ADHD?

No, you don't outgrow it. Adults can have ADD or ADHD too, but as teens get older, the symptoms may be less severe. The brain matures with age which means many skills such as organization will improve with time. Teens also learn new skills to help them cope better. For example, Alex uses a pocket PC (iPAQ) to help him remember assignments, appointments and deadlines such as paying his rent on time. Now that he understands his attention deficit, he knows he has problems with his memory, so he has learned to take charge and develop a system to help him remember important things. The good news is that life does get better as you get older.

Appendix 4: _____

The ADD/ADHD Iceberg

Attention deficit disorder may be compared to an iceberg: *most of the problems are hidden beneath the surface and only the tip of the problem is visible!* Typically, teachers and parents see the obvious tip first: the behavior problems, such as failing to complete homework, talking back, and arguing. Yet for so many teenagers, an attention deficit is much more complex than just these obvious behaviors. School is often incredibly challenging because of your inattention, disorganization, executive function deficits and other serious learning problems. Remember, two-thirds of you have at least one other diagnosable condition that often has a significant impact on your schoolwork.

When you think of attention deficit disorder, visualize this iceberg with only one-eighth of its mass visible above the water line. As is true of icebergs, often the most challenging aspects of ADD and ADHD lurk beneath the surface. For example, take a minute and look at all the characteristics listed below the surface. Do you have problems falling asleep or waking up, getting somewhere on time, repeating misbehavior, memorizing multiplication tables, or getting started on your schoolwork? All these things often go along with your attention deficit. Most people don't understand just how complex ADD and ADHD are, and how difficult it is for you to cope with it. You may want to show this iceberg to your parents or teachers. It may help them understand attention deficits better.

THE ADD/ADHD ICEBERG
Only 1/8 of an iceberg is visible!!
Most of it is hidden beneath the surface!!

THE TIP OF THE ICEBERG:
The Obvious ADD/ADHD Behaviors

IMPULSIVITY
Lacks self-control   Difficulty awaiting turn
Blurts out   Interrupts
Tells untruths   Intrudes
Talks back   Loses temper

HYPERACTIVITY
Restless   Talks a lot
Fidgets   Can't sit still
Runs or climbs a lot   Always on the go

INATTENTION
Disorganized   Doesn't follow through
Doesn't pay attention   Is forgetful
Doesn't seem to listen   Distractible
Makes careless mistakes   Loses things
Doesn't do school work

HIDDEN BENEATH THE SURFACE:
The Not So Obvious Behaviors!!

NEUROTRANSMITTER DEFICITS IMPACT BEHAVIOR
Inefficient levels of neurotransmitters,
dpamine, norepinephrine, & serotonin,
result in reduced brain activity
on thinking tasks.

WEAK EXECUTIVE FUNCTIONING
Working Memory and Recall
Activation, Alertness, and Effort
Internalizing language
Controlling emotions
Complex Problem Solving

IMPAIRED SENSE OF TIME
Doesn't judge passage of time accurately
Loses track of time
Often late
Doesn't have skills to plan ahead
Forgets long-term projects or is late
Difficulty estimating time required for tasks
Difficulty planning for future
Impatient
Hates waiting
Time creeps
Homework takes forever
Avoids doing homework

SLEEP DISTURBANCE (56%)
Doesn't get restful sleep
Can't fall asleep
Can't wake up
Late for school
Sleeps in class
Sleep deprived
Irritable
Morning battles with parents

FOUR TO SIX YEAR DEVELOPMENTAL DELAY
Less mature (30% delay)
Less responsible
18 yr. old acts like 12

NOT LEARNING EASILY FROM REWARDS AND PUNISHMENT
Repeats misbehavior
May be difficult to discipline
Less likely to follow rules
Difficulty managing his own behavior
Doesn't study past behavior
Doesn't learn from past behavior
Acts without sense of hindsight
Must have immediate rewards
Long-term rewards don't work
Doesn't examine his own behavior
Difficulty changing his behavior

COEXISTING CONDITIONS
2/3 have at least one other condition
Anxiety (34%)   Depression (29%)
Bipolar (12%)   Substance Abuse (5-40%)
Tourette Disorder (11%)
Obsessive Compulsive Disorder (4%)
Oppositional Defiant Disorder (54-67%)
Conduct Disorder (22-43%)

SERIOUS LEARNING PROBLEMS (90%)
Specific Learning Disability (25-50%)
Poor working memory   Can't memorize easily
Forgets teacher and parent requests
Slow math calculation (26%)
Spelling Problems (24%)
Poor written expression (65%)
Difficulty writing essays
Slow retrieval of information
Poor listening and reading comprehension
Difficulty describing the world in words
Difficulty rapidly putting words together
Disorganization
Slow cognitive processing speed
Poor fine motor coordination
Poor handwriting
Inattention   Impulsive learning style

LOW FRUSTRATION TOLERANCE
Difficulty Controlling Emotions
Short fuse   Emotionally reactive
Loses temper easily
May give up more easily
Doesn't stick with things
Speaks or acts before thinking
Concerned with own feelings
Difficulty seeing others perspective
May be self-centered
May be selfish

••••••••••••••
ADD/ADHD is often more complex than most people realize!
Like icebergs, many problems related to ADD/ADHD are not visible. ADD/ADHD may be mild, moderate, or severe,
is likely to coexist with other conditions, and may be a disability for some students.

© 2003 Alex Zeigler

Reprinted from *Teaching Teens with ADD and ADHD,* 2000.
Revised by Zeigler and Dendy. Artwork by Zeigler.
©2003

Appendix 5: _____

What Do I Need to Know about My Brain?

How Your Brain Helps You Pay Attention!

These explanations are oversimplified, but they will give you an idea of what scientists believe may cause inattention.

When a teacher says, "Open your book to page 37 and work the first ten math problems," it sounds like a pretty simple request. In reality, your brain must perform some pretty complex actions before you can actually start working on your math problems.

Let me see if I can explain this complicated process in a way that's easy to understand. Once a student hears a message, it must be sent along several million of the neurons in your brain. You hear the message, then your brain processes the information and sends messages in the form of an electrical current to all the appropriate places for a response. Finally, the message is sent to your hands to actually open the book and start working the math problems.

One of the key steps is for the teacher's message to move along the network of neurons known as the **neural network** in your brain by jumping from one neuron to the next. As you can see in the diagram on the next page, each message (electrical current) moves down the **axon** until it reaches the nerve endings. If you look more closely, you will see that the neurons don't touch each other. They are separated by a space known as a **synaptic cleft** or **synapse**. The second neuron has **receptor sites** that have "electrical switches" so that they can receive the message. Next the message must find a way to turn on the electrical switch so that it can cross from one neuron to the next one.

Once the electrical current reaches the nerve endings, it releases **neurotransmitters** (chemical messengers of the brain) such as *dopamine*, into the synaptic cleft so they can carry the message across. These neurotransmitters help the receptors on the second neuron to fire—take the message and pass it along to other neurons. Once the message is received by the second neuron, the dopamine is broken down and taken back up into the first neuron to wait for the next message to come along. When describing this process to his patients, Dr. Ted Mandelkorn, a veteran pediatrician, explains that it's like having a dump truck sitting in the synapse waiting to recycle the dopamine after the message is delivered to the second neuron. In other words, the dopamine is recycled and used again.

The neurotransmitters, *norepinephrine* and *serotonin*, are also a very important part of the neurotransmitter recycling system and act in similar ways to dopamine when they move into the synapse to pass along messages.

Remember these facts as you read the next paragraph: *messages can't move across the synapse unless the right amount of a neurotransmitter like dopamine stays in the synaptic cleft* for a while. Neurotransmitters must work properly before you can do as the teacher asks.

Here's What Experts Think Happens in Students with ADD or ADHD!

Experts believe the major reason we can't pay attention is because we don't have enough dopamine and norepinephrine in all our brain circuits. When the teacher's message reaches the synapse, the dopamine moves out into the synaptic cleft. However, the dopamine is broken down too quickly and the **dopamine transporters** take it back into the neuron before the message can cross the synapse. Scientists refer to these dopamine transporters as *DAT1.* In fact, scientists tell us that some people with ADHD have *70 percent more dopamine transporters* than people without ADHD. That's like having two recycling dump trucks in the synapse whereas most people have only one truck. As a result there is not enough dopamine left for messages from the teacher to cross the synapse. When this happens, the teacher may think the student is not paying attention or not trying, but in truth, the brain chemicals are not working quite right. When the neurotransmitters work right, the electrical switch in the **dopamine receptors** (*DRD2 and DRD4*) is turned on and the message is sent to the next neuron. Then the teenager is able to pay attention.

So, as Dr. Mandelkorn explains, you're sending all the right messages, but they can't always get across the synapse (not turning in homework, forgetting to do chores, etc.). To fix this we need to *slow down the neurotransmitter recycling system* so the dopamine can trigger the electrical switch and pass along messages.

Dr. Mandelkorn assures his patients there is nothing wrong with their brain cells; they work just fine. He explains that their inattention is caused by problems with a faulty neurotransmitter recycling system that operates between brain cells.

Another gene that is also present in some teens with attention deficits is linked to daring behavior. Students who have this gene are more likely to take risks.

How Does Medication Help Your Brain Pay Attention?

Have you ever wondered how medicine helps your brain work better? Here is what the experts believe is happening. When you take medications like Adderall, Concerta, Ritalin, or Strattera, they make the neurotransmitters in your brain work better:

➤ the dopamine and norepinephrine stay out in the synaptic cleft longer
➤ the electrical switch is turned on at receptor sites
➤ consequently, messages can move across the synapse to the next neuron.

That means it's a lot easier to pay attention and do what teachers ask you to do.

Of course, you already know that medicine is not a magic bullet. You will still have to work very hard and learn new skills so you can compensate for your attention deficit.

The Link between Neurons, Neurotransmitters, and Attention

The simplified drawing in Figure 1 shows how scientists think your brain helps you pay attention. For easier display, the neuron in the diagram is divided in half to show how neurotransmitters work in the brains of two different people. One side shows how the neuron works in a person who does *not* have ADHD and the other shows how it works when ADHD is present.

➤ In **Neuron 1** (without ADHD) on the next page, neurotransmitters turn on the switch at the receptor site which allows messages to cross the synapse.
➤ In **Neuron 2** (with ADHD), the neurotransmitters break down and are taken back up into the neuron before they can turn on the switch at the receptor site. Consequently, messages can't cross the synapse.
➤ Medication helps keep the right amount of neurotransmitters in the synapse. That's why medicine helps you pay attention!

Figure 1:

Neurons, Neurotransmitters, and Attention

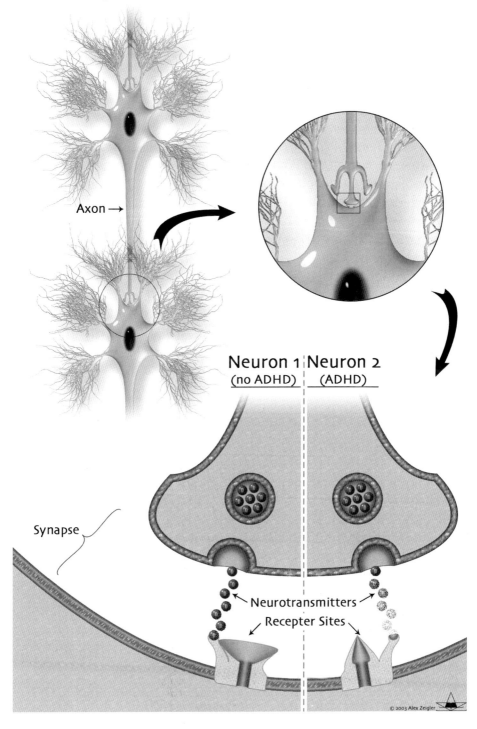

© 2003 Alex Zeigler

Appendix 6: _____

What Do I Need to Know about Medication?

The main reason to take medicine is to help the chemicals in your brain work right. When that happens, you can pay attention, do your schoolwork, and get along better with your friends, parents and teachers. Most of us wish we didn't have to take medicine, but over the years we've learned we really need to take it so we can do our best in school. One of the hardest things to do, however, is to get the medicine right. Here are several questions and answers that may help you understand medication better.

1. What medication should I take for my attention deficit?

Most teenagers who take medicine for their attention deficit end up taking a *stimulant medication*. That's just a shorter way of saying a central nervous system stimulant medication. Basically they gave the medicine that name because it stimulates the central nervous system so that the neurotransmitters work better and you can pay attention.

Most stimulant medications are made out of one of two major chemicals, *methylphenidate* or *amphetamine*. Examples of medicines with a methylphenidate base include Ritalin and Concerta. Dexedrine and Adderall are examples of amphetamines. These medicines are usually given two names, a generic and a brand name. For example, methylphenidate is the generic name, a broad general name given to the medicine; Ritalin is a brand name, the specific name the company gives to the medication. As you know, these medicines may last from three to twelve hours, depending on which one is taken. These types of medicines help the neurotransmitter *dopamine* work better. Adderall, however, affects both *dopamine* and *norepinephrine*.

The most commonly used stimulant medications are Ritalin, Adderall, Adderall XR and Concerta. Other stimulants include Ritalin SR, Ritalin LA, Metadate, Dexedrine, Dexedrine SR, Methylin, and Focalin. Some parents prefer brand name medicines, believing they work better than generic meds. Generics, however, work just fine for some students.

Strattera is another medicine that you might take. What makes Strattera special is that it is *not* a stimulant medication. Strattera came out in 2002, and it's the first new type of medication in thirty years for treating attention deficits. Researchers are excited because Strattera may last all day whereas the longest most stimulants last is ten to twelve hours. Only time will tell if Strattera will last a full twenty-four hours.

Strattera could be important to you for several reasons. For example, it works in the morning when you wake up and is still working at night when you go to bed. In addition, it will be easier to get a refill of your medicine; the doctor can call your prescription in to the pharmacy. In fact, your doctor can even give you some samples so you can see if it works for you. Instead of the neurotransmitter dopamine, this medication helps *norepinephrine* work better.

Of course, Strattera has not been researched as well as methylphenidates and amphetamines. So keep reading the research on this medication because the jury is still out on just exactly how effective it will be and whether or not future research will find any serious negative side effects.

2. How does medicine work?

When you take a medication like Ritalin, Adderall or Concerta, neurotransmitters work better in key parts of your brain. As a result, the blood flow and activity also increase and you can pay attention to messages from your parents and teachers. As we explained in Appendix 5, as messages travel through the brain, they have to jump across the synapse between the neurons. Your neurotransmitters make it possible for messages to cross the synapse. The bottom line is you can pay attention and do better schoolwork.

3. How long does medication last?

Stimulant medications can be divided into three groups based upon how long they last. One group that includes Ritalin (5 mg) and Dexedrine (10 mg) is called *short-acting* because it lasts roughly three hours. The next or *intermediate group* includes medicines like Adderall, Metadate ER, and Ritalin SR that last about five to eight hours. Then the *long-acting* medicines like Adderall XR, Concerta, Ritalin LA, and Metadate CD will last up to twelve hours. Doctors sometimes call these "clean medications" because they have few side effects and are in and out of your body fairly quickly. Typically, all of these medications are gone from your body within 24 hours. Of course, the new non-stimulant, Strattera, lasts all day.

4. How do you know when medication works right?

You'll see specific changes in the way you act. One way you can tell is if you're listening to the teacher, finishing your work, and making better grades. Some students can't always tell when they act differently, so their teachers or parents may have to tell them.

Here are some changes you should see when your medicine works right:

Several problems get better. You can
- pay attention better
- concentrate better
- work harder at school
- get along better with friends and adults
- do more schoolwork
- make better grades

Parents and teachers also see that you
- are less hyperactive
- aren't as impulsive
- don't argue and talk back as much
- aren't as angry or aggressive

Since medication usually wears off by the time you get home, your parents may not really know if your medicine is working right. You and your teacher are probably in the best position to know how well your medicine is working. If you and your teacher don't see these changes, then you and your parents should talk with your doctor. There is a medication rating scale in Appendix 7 that you, your parents and your teacher can complete. Then you can take the results to the doctor to help him or her know how to help you.

5. Is it okay to combine medicines?

Doctors don't like to do this very often, but sometimes it can be helpful. For example, some doctors may give a small dose of a short-acting medicine at the end of the day when your extended-release medicine has worn off. This will help you make it through your evening homework. For those who are still taking Ritalin SR, some doctors have found that it works better if you combine the Ritalin SR and a short-acting Ritalin.

Doctors can also combine medicines that have the same medicine base, such as methylphenidates or amphetamines. That's why doctors can give you a small dose of Ritalin or Focalin (5-10 mgs) to go with an earlier Ritalin SR, Metadate, or Concerta. Or they can give you Dexedrine (5 mgs) if you have taken Dexedrine SR or Adderall earlier in the day.

6. What are these other medications my doctor wants me to take?

If you're anxious, depressed, impulsive, having major trouble sleeping, or are extremely irritable or aggressive, your doctor may suggest counseling or even taking an additional medication. For example, your doctor may recommend other medicines like Zoloft, Wellbutrin, or Effexor. Other medicines that are used less often include Prozac, Celexa, Tofranil, Norpramin, Depakote, or clonidine. If you're having sleep problems, the doctor may prescribe clonidine, Trazadone, Remeron, or Atarax. Zyprexa and Seroquel are stronger medicines and are used less often to help with sleep.

7. Will I get addicted if I take these medications?

Obviously, there probably have been some people who have abused these medications and become addicted. In reality, experts tell us that students who take these medicines like the doctor tells them, are unlikely to have any major problems. When you have an attention deficit, these medicines don't make you high; they help you settle down and pay attention. Experts also tell us that the abuse of medicines like Ritalin or Dexedrine tends to be done by others, not by students who have a prescription for it.

In the past, a few people have abused stimulants and become addicted, so the government felt that it had to control their sale and use. The government calls these medicines *Schedule II controlled substances,* which sounds a little scary. That's why the doctor has to write out a new prescription every month and can't just call in a refill to the drug store. That's also why Strattera offers a promising alternative for families; it's not a Schedule II medication and appears to have little potential for drug abuse. Some parents who may have been afraid of stimulants before may be willing to try Strattera.

Some people mistakenly think that the stimulant medications are bad just because they're called stimulants or Schedule II medicines. They're afraid that you might become addicted. But experts tell us that's not true. If fact, most of you are no more likely to get addicted to drugs than your friends. As we explained earlier, you're *less likely to abuse drugs* than other students who have attention deficits and don't take medicine when they need it.

If for some reason, you can't take medicine, we don't want you to be afraid that you may become a drug addict. As explained earlier, you can work with your parents and other adults to do everything else listed in "Getting Treatment Right" to make certain you aren't tempted by illegal drugs.

When I have asked teenagers who take Ritalin or Adderall if they're addicted, they all say, "No!" In fact, they really don't want to take medicine. I bet you know there is *no risk* of you abusing or getting addicted to your ADD/ADHD medication. Here is the reason I say that. When you wake up first thing in the morning, do you jump out of bed and say, "I can't wait to take my medicine?" Do you find yourself saying, "I can't wait to take my next pill?" I didn't think so. In fact, I bet you would prefer not to take any medicine at all if you could do okay in school without it.

8. Will taking a stimulant medication like Ritalin keep me from getting into the military?

Let me begin by saying that teenagers who are successful in the military typically loved ROTC in high school and always knew they wanted to go into the armed services. Of course there are many other teens with attention deficits who will not join any branch of the service because they hate the thought of dealing with the rigid discipline of the military.

Because the military has some misconceptions about attention deficits and stimulant medications, they say they don't want you taking these medicines at least a year before joining most branches of the service. Some people who have attention deficits, however, join the armed forces and do very well. Several things about the military make it easier for a teenager with an attention deficit to be successful, even without medication. They provide a lot of structure—someone always tells you what to do and when to do it—and you're getting lots of exercise, which helps your brain work better.

Because Strattera is not a stimulant medication and should not show up in drug tests, teenagers may be able to take it when they enter the military. However, this medicine is still so new that it's too early to say for a fact that this will be true.

We have to honestly say that being diagnosed with an attention deficit could cause some problems later with the military, including most of the military academies like the Naval Academy and West Point. In addition, Matthew Cohen, a special education attorney and former CHADD president, indicated that the military has refused to accept people who took stimulants and has discharged others for using these medications. In fact, after being injured during basic training, one teen told the doctor about his ADHD. Even though he was doing well in training and had not taken medication since high school, he was released from the military because of "failure to disclose" his ADHD.

However, we also know two teens with attention deficits who went into the Marines and did well. They were not taking stimulants for at least a year before they enlisted. Decisions were made for them and their lives were so structured that they didn't need medication on a daily basis. Of course these restrictions seem discriminatory and unfair, but you can't win when you argue with the government.

9. Will taking a stimulant medication keep me from getting a job?

When you get older and apply for a job, stimulant medicines may show up in some drug tests. In most situations, as long as you can show them that your doctor has given you a prescription for it, there should not be any problems that you can't work out with your employer.

One really difficult decision you'll have to make is whether or not to declare your attention deficit as a disability in hopes of getting accommodations on the job such as more frequent supervision, assistance with paper work, or time management training. Some people decide not to tell their employer about their attention deficit.

Special education attorney Matthew Cohen has found that sometimes when you tell an employer about your attention deficit, they may find some other reason not to hire you or to fire you. However, in reality they don't want you because of your attention deficit. Of course, these actions are discriminatory and unfair but you may not be able to do anything about it short of filing a lawsuit. Even then there are no guarantees that you'll win your case.

According to Cohen, you are only entitled to reasonable accommodations under the Americans with Disabilities Act (ADA) *if* you disclose your disability, request specific reasonable accommodations and provide documentation both of the disability and the need for the accommodations. This means each person has to weigh the need for accommodations in relation to any potential negative consequences of disclosure. Consultation with an attorney who specializes in this area is often useful in making a decision.

Having an attention deficit isn't always a bad thing on the job. One of my friends was hired at a radio station and in talking with his boss found out that they were both taking Adderall. Each situation is different. You need to find a job where the characteristics of your attention deficit are less likely to interfere, for example, a salesman, landscape contractor, or emergency medical technician.

If you have problems once you get a job, you may find it helpful to talk with your boss about specific skills you're struggling with rather than say you have ADD or ADHD, especially if your bosses don't understand the condition. For example if your boss has been critical of your lack of paper work, you might say, "I have trouble with time management and getting my paper work done on time. Here are some things I'm doing to try to correct the problem. I'm going to put my deadlines into my Palm Pilot so I'll be reminded when my paper work is due. I'll also get my secretary to help me with some of the more routine paper work." Or to help you reduce written work, you could develop a form like a checklist that would be faster than writing out a full report.

Or if you're having trouble getting to work on time, you may work out a system on your own so you're on time. For example, you may set your alarm thirty minutes earlier. You may have to talk with your doctor about your sleep disturbance and ask for help getting restful sleep and waking up more easily. These are examples of how you can learn to take charge of your attention deficit and your life.

Your attention deficit may be a disability in school
but it does not have to be a disability in life!

Appendix 7:
A Medication Rating Scale

Name:_____Date & class:_____

Completed by:_____Time of day observed:_____

To assess the impact medication is having on a student's schoolwork, each teacher should answer several key questions. When medication is working properly and learning problems have been identified, the student should be doing much better in school. If the teacher cannot check the "Strongly agree" and "Agree" columns, then problems may still exist in several areas: 1) the proper accommodations are not being provided for the student's learning problems, 2) executive function deficits are not being addressed, or 3) the medication regimen may not be right for the student. Please circle the answer that best describes the student's behavior.

__Academic Performance:__	Strongly agree	Agree	Neutral	Disagree	Strongly disagree
When the student is in my class, s/he:					
1. pays attention	1	2	3	4	5
2. completes class and homework	1	2	3	4	5
3. does work correctly	1	2	3	4	5
4. complies with requests	1	2	3	4	5
5. makes passing grades	1	2	3	4	5

ADD/ADHD-Related Behaviors, Including Executive Function

If the student is on medication and is not doing well in school, what else could be causing continuing problems? Are there any ADD/ADHD-related behaviors that are interfering with the student's ability to succeed in school?

__ADD/ADHD-Related Behaviors:__	Strongly agree	Agree	Neutral	Disagree	Strongly disagree
The student					
6. is organized	1	2	3	4	5
7. manages time well	1	2	3	4	5
8. remembers things easily	1	2	3	4	5
9. is on time to class	1	2	3	4	5
10. is on time to school	1	2	3	4	5
11. thinks carefully before act or speaking	1	2	3	4	5
12. is awake and alert in class	1	2	3	4	5
Ask parents about any sleep problems. The teenager					
13. falls asleep easily	1	2	3	4	5
14. wakes up easily	1	2	3	4	5

Comments: _____

If problems still exist, should a behavioral intervention plan be developed to 1) identify hidden learning problems, 2) provide additional accommodations, 3) teach the student compensatory skills, or 4) should teachers suggest that parents seek medical advice? (Reprinted from *Teaching Teens with ADD and ADHD* (2000), Dendy.)

Appendix 8: _____

Executive Function...
"What is this anyway?"

Published as "5 Components of Executive Function" in CHADD's
ATTENTION Magazine, February 2002

Parents and teachers are often baffled when students with
attention deficits, including those who are intellectually gifted, teeter
on the brink of school failure. Recently researchers may have solved
part of this challenging puzzle; deficits in critical cognitive skills,
known as *executive function,* may interfere with a student's ability to
succeed in school. Practically speaking, executive function deficits may
cause problems for students with ADD or ADHD in several important
areas: getting started and finishing work, remembering homework,
memorizing facts, writing essays or reports, working math problems,
being on time, controlling emotions, completing long-term projects,
and planning for the future.

Although scientists have not yet agreed on the exact elements
of executive function, two leading researchers on Attention Deficit
Disorder, Dr. Russell Barkley and Dr. Tom Brown, have given us
insightful working descriptions. Dr. Barkley describes executive
function as those "actions we perform to ourselves and direct at
ourselves so as to accomplish self-control, goal-directed behavior, and
the maximization of future outcomes." Through use of a metaphor, Dr.
Brown gives us a helpful visual image by comparing executive function
to the conductor's role in an orchestra. The conductor organizes
various instruments to begin playing singularly or in combination,
integrates the music by bringing in and fading certain actions, and
controls the pace and intensity of the music.

Although the impact of executive function deficits on school
success is profound, this fact is often unrecognized by many parents
and teachers. I learned the hard way with my own son that a high IQ
score alone was not enough to make good grades. Early in my son's
academic career, I knew something was interfering with his ability to

do well in school. But it wasn't until Dr. Barkley identified the central role executive function plays in school success, that I finally understood why school was so difficult for him.

Components of Executive Function

Based upon material from Barkley and Brown, I have outlined five general components of executive function that impact school performance:

❶ **Working memory and recall** (holding facts in mind while manipulating information; accessing facts stored in long-term memory.)

❷ **Activation, arousal, and effort** (getting started; paying attention; finishing work)

❸ **Controlling emotions** (ability to tolerate frustration; thinking before acting or speaking)

❹ **Internalizing language** (using "self-talk" to control one's behavior and direct future actions)

❺ **Taking an issue apart, analyzing the pieces, reconstituting and organizing it into new ideas** (complex problem solving).

Let's take a more in-depth look at just one element of executive function—deficits in working memory and recall—and their impact on school work.

Poor Working Memory and Recall

❶ Affects the *here and now:*
  ➤ limited working memory capacity
  ➤ weak short-term memory (holding information in mind for roughly twenty seconds; capacity—roughly the equivalent of seven numbers)
  ➤ forgetfulness—can't keep several things in mind
    As a result, students:
    ➤ have difficulty remembering and following instructions.
    ➤ have difficulty memorizing math facts, spelling words, and dates.
    ➤ have difficulty performing mental computation such as math in one's head.
    ➤ forget one part of a problem while working on another segment.
    ➤ have difficulty paraphrasing or summarizing.

❷ Affects their sense of *past events:*
  ➤ difficulty recalling the past

> As a result, students:
>> ➤ do not learn easily from past behavior (limited hindsight).
>> ➤ repeat misbehavior.

3) <u>Affects their sense of *time:*</u>
> ➤ difficulty holding events in mind
> ➤ difficulty using their sense of time to prepare for upcoming events and the future
>
> <u>As a result, students:</u>
>> ➤ have difficulty judging the passage of time accurately.
>> ➤ do not accurately estimate how much time it will take to finish a task; consequently, they may not allow enough time to complete work.

4) <u>Affects their sense of *self-awareness*</u>
> ➤ diminished sense of self-awareness
>
> <u>As a result, students:</u>
>> ➤ do not easily examine or change their own behavior.

5) <u>Affects their sense of the *future*:</u>
> ➤ students live in the present—focus on the here and now
> ➤ less likely to talk about time or plan for the future
>
> <u>As a result, students:</u>
>> ➤ have difficulty projecting lessons learned in the past, forward into the future (limited foresight).
>> ➤ have difficulty preparing for the future.

Common Academic Problems Linked to ADHD and Executive Function Deficits

Many students with ADD or ADHD have **impaired working memory** and **slow processing speed,** which are important elements of executive function. Not surprisingly, these skills are critical for writing essays and working math problems.

A recent research study by Mayes and Calhoun has identified **written expression** as the most common learning problem among students with ADHD (65 percent). Consequently, writing essays, drafting book reports or answering questions on tests or homework is often very challenging for these students. For example, when writing essays, students often have difficulty holding ideas in mind, acting upon and organizing ideas, quickly retrieving grammar, spelling and punctuation rules from long-term memory, manipulating all this information, remembering ideas to write down, organizing the material in a logical sequence, and then reviewing and correcting errors.

Since learning is relatively easy for most of us, sometimes we forget just how complex seemingly simple tasks such as memorizing multiplication tables or working a math problem really are. For example, when a student works on a math problem, he must fluidly move back and forth between analytical skills and several levels of memory (working, short-term, and long-term memory). With word problems, he must hold several numbers and questions in mind while he decides how to work a problem. Next he must delve into long-term memory to find the correct math rule to use for the problem. Then he must hold important facts in mind while he applies the rules and shifts information back and forth between working and short-term memory to work the problem and determine the answer.

To further complicate matters, other serious conditions may co-occur with ADD and ADHD. According to the recent landmark National Institute of Mental Health *MTA Study, two thirds of children with ADHD have at least one other coexisting problem, such as depression or anxiety.* Accommodating students with complex cases of attention deficit disorder is critical! These children are at greater risk than their peers for a multitude of school problems, for example, failing a grade, skipping school, suspension, expulsion, and sometimes, dropping out of school and not going to college.

Favorite School Success Strategies

Over the years I have collected several favorite teaching strategies and accommodations that work well for students with ADD or ADHD. So here are just a few of my favorite tips:

General Teaching Strategies

➤ **Make the learning process as concrete and visual as possible.**

<u>Written expression</u>

➤ Dictate information to a "scribe" or parents.

➤ Use graphic organizers to provide visual prompts.

➤ Use Post-it notes to brainstorm essay ideas.

<u>Math</u>

➤ Use paired learning (teacher explains problem, students make up their own examples, swap problems, and discuss and correct answers).

➤ Use a peer tutor.

(After barely passing high school and college algebra, my son made an A in calculus plus had a 100 average on tests when the professor used this strategy. At the same time, he also tutored a friend.)

Memory

> Use mnemonics (memory tricks), such as acronyms or acrostics, e.g., HOMES to remember names of the Great Lakes, Huron, Ontario, Michigan, Erie, and Superior.
> Use visual posting of key information on strips of poster board.

> **Modify teaching methods.**

> Use an overhead projector to demonstrate how to write an essay. (Parents may simply write on paper or a computer to model this skill.)
> Use color to highlight important information.
> Use graphic organizers to help students organize their thoughts.

> **Modify assignments–reduce written work.**

> Shorten assignments.
> Check time spent on homework, and reduce it if appropriate (when total homework takes longer than roughly 10 minutes per grade level as recommended in a PTA/NEA Policy, e.g. 7th grader = 70 minutes).
> Write answers only, not the questions (photocopy questions).

> **Modify testing and grading.**

> Give extended time on tests.
> Divide long-term projects into segments with separate due dates and grades.
> Average two grades on essays– one for content and one for grammar.

> **Modify level of support and supervision.**

> Appoint a "row captain" to check to see that homework assignments are written down and later turned in to the teacher.
> Increase the amount of supervision and monitoring for these students, if they're struggling.

> **Use technology.**

> Use a computer as often as possible.
> Use software to help teach skills.

Unfortunately students with ADD or ADHD are often punished for executive function deficits such as lack of organizational and memory skills that interfere with their ability to bring home the correct homework assignments and books. Hopefully, after reading this article, teachers and parents will develop more innovative intervention strategies. For example, one effective alternative would be to have someone (a friend or teacher aide), meet the student at his locker to get the necessary homework materials together. Ultimately, this process of *modeling* and *shaping* behavior at the critical *point of performance* will help the student master skills or at a minimum, teach him to compensate for deficits.

In Closing

Clearly school is often very difficult for students with attention deficits. However, when executive function deficits are also present, the accompanying problems are often overwhelming to the student and family. Unfortunately, some parents and teachers have had little awareness or sympathy for the challenges presented by these combined deficits. Hopefully, teachers and parents now realize that attention deficit disorder is often a very complex condition! It's much more than just a simple case of hyperactivity. When deficits in executive function and related learning problems are present, *students can try their very best and still not succeed in school!*

So what should parents and teachers do with this new information?

Identify:

❶   the student's *specific learning problems* (e.g. written expression or math) and

❷   their *executive function deficits* (e.g. working memory, disorganization, forgetfulness, or impaired sense of time) and

❸   **provide accommodations in both areas!**

I leave you with this food for thought,

Succeeding in school is one of the most therapeutic things that can happen to a child!
So do whatever it takes to help the child succeed in school.

On a personal note, our youngest son struggled terribly throughout his school years with ADD inattentive and executive function issues. Although college was incredibly difficult, Alex recently graduated with a degree in Forensics. We're so proud of him and his tenacity. So if your child is struggling in school, do not give up. My family offers living proof that there is hope and help for ADHD and coexisting conditions.

Please visit my website www.chrisdendy.com to learn more about my family and how we've coped with ADD and ADHD. Several helpful articles are also available for you to download and share with friends. Best wishes for school success to you, your children and students with attention deficits!

See the original article for references including Barkley, Brown, Dendy, Deshler, Levine, Mayes and Calhoun.

For more information contact CHADD at 8181 Professional Place, Suite 201, Landover, MD 20875; www.chadd.org; 18002334050

Appendix 9: _____

A Graphic Organizer
for Writing an Essay

I. Thesis Paragraph (Topic – mentors)
   A. Definition _____
   B. Importance _____
   C. Three key traits _____ _____ _____

II. First Supporting Paragraph
   A. Topic sentence (1st trait) _____
   B. Supporting examples _____
   _____
   C. Transition to next paragraph _____

III. Second Supporting Paragraph
   A. Topic sentence (2nd key trait) _____
   B. Supporting examples _____
   _____
   C. Transition to next paragraph _____

IV. Third Supporting Paragraph
   A. Topic sentence (3rd key trait) _____
   B. Supporting examples _____
   _____

V. Conclusion
   A. Restate importance of having a mentor
   _____
   B. Restate the three key character traits
   _____ _____ _____
   C. Explain what a difference a mentor would make in your life
   _____

(Reprinted from *Teaching Teens with ADD and ADHD* (2000), Dendy.)

Appendix 10:

ADD & ADHD Dictionary

accommodation: If your attention deficit interferes with your ability to learn, most schools will provide special supports or make adjustments to help you be successful. For example, if you read and process information slowly, the school may shorten your homework assignments or give you extra time on tests.

ADA: Stands for the Americans with Disabilities Act, a federal disability law. This law is often thought of in terms of work place discrimination. However, it also applies to all state and local governments and to all places of public accommodation, including private schools and colleges that are not affiliated with religious institutions. Under certain conditions, eligible students or adults may receive reasonable accommodations under this act.

ADD: Stands for attention deficit disorder. Students with ADD inattentive have trouble paying attention, are forgetful, lose things, appear not to listen, have trouble getting organized, and may read and write more slowly than other students. However, they're definitely not hyperactive. In fact, they may be almost the exact opposite: they may be low-key and laid back. Typically they don't have as much energy as students with ADHD and some may be called couch potatoes. They may be known as daydreamers or space cadets. Teachers call this condition ADD and doctors call it AD/HD, predominately inattentive. Experts sometimes use the term "slow cognitive tempo," to describe this type of attention deficit.

ADHD: Stands for attention deficit hyperactivity disorder. Three key characteristics are found in people with ADHD—inattention, impulsivity, and hyperactivity. These teenagers may also talk a lot, interrupt people who are talking, and may be restless instead of hyperactive. See Appendix 3 for information on both ADD and ADHD. Sometimes ADD and ADHD are used interchangeably to include everyone with an attention deficit.

ADHD coach: A person specifically trained to help children, teenagers or adults cope with the challenges of having an attention deficit. Typically, a coach is different from a tutor; a tutor tends to teach academic information, whereas a coach may help you be better organized, find ways to remember things, and manage your time better. A coach will teach you new skills and strategies for compensating for your attention deficit. Often a parent or a good friend may act as a coach for a teenager. When you become an adult, you may decide to hire an ADHD coach.

Adderall: A brand name extended-release stimulant medication that helps students pay attention. One of the main ingredients in Adderall is amphetamine. Although there are two forms of Adderall, this one usually lasts six to eight hours.

Adderall XR: A long-acting stimulant medication that helps students pay attention. Like regular Adderall, one of the main ingredients in Adderall XR is amphetamine. This medicine, however, lasts longer—ten to twelve hours.

amphetamine: A chemical that is used in Adderall, Adderall XR, Dexedrine, and Dexedrine SR that helps students to pay attention and concentrate.

antidepressant: A medication used to treat depression in adults. In children and teenagers, however, it is used to treat anxiety, obsessive-compulsive disorder, irritability and aggression. Although it does help reduce inattention and hyperactivity, it's not nearly as good as a stimulant medication. Consequently, it's considered a medication of second choice in treatment of attention deficits. Antidepressants increase the level of serotonin, a neurotransmitter, in the brain. Thus, the person may feel better, have more energy, and be less irritable or angry.

Aricept: A medication for Alzheimer's patients that experts have found helps improve memory in some patients with an attention deficit.

axon: Part of a nerve cell along which impulses (messages) travel.

brand name medication: The specific name the company gives to a medicine, for example Ritalin is a brand name of methylphenidate.

clonidine: The generic name of a medicine also known by the brand name of Catapres. This medicine is used to treat ADHD, tic disorders, and sleep problems in children. When used alone or in combination with a stimulant like Ritalin, it can be effective in helping teenagers with *severe hyperactivity or aggression.* In addition, it may reduce anxiety and restlessness. In adults, it's used to treat high blood pressure. Tenex is similar to clonidine, but has fewer side effects (less sedation so you don't get as sleepy).

coexisting condition: Medical conditions that occur in addition to ADD or ADHD. Most students with an attention deficit also have other conditions, such as anxiety or learning disabilities. In fact, experts from a major National Institute Mental Health (NIMH) study say that 69 percent of children with ADHD have at least one other coexisting condition. Doctors call this a *comorbid condition.* But my family hates that word since it sounds terrible—so we call it a coexisting condition instead.

Concerta: A brand name long-acting stimulant medication that helps students pay attention. Like Ritalin, one of the main ingredients in Concerta is methylphenidate. It usually lasts ten to twelve hours.

Depakote: The brand name of a medicine also known by the generic name of valproic acid. Depakote is an antiseizure medication that is helpful in treating angry, aggressive behavior and mood swings. Although it can be used in treatment of ADHD, it's the medication prescribed most often for treating bipolar disorder in youth.

developmental delay: According to researchers, teenagers with attention deficits mature later than teens who don't have ADD or ADHD. These teens show roughly a thirty percent delay in their maturity levels. So an 18 year old may act more like a 12-year-old.

Dexedrine: A brand name stimulant medication that helps students pay attention. One of the main ingredients in Dexedrine is amphetamine. It usually lasts three to four hours.

Dexedrine SR: A sustained-release stimulant medication that helps students pay attention. One of the main ingredients in Dexedrine is amphetamine. It usually lasts six to eight hours.

dopamine: A neurotransmitter in the brain that allows students to pay attention by helping messages cross from one neuron to the next. After a message gets across the synapse, the dopamine is sucked back up into its home neuron and waits to carry the next message across. See the diagram in Appendix 5.

dopamine receptor (DRD): The site on the receiving neuron that dopamine activates so that it can receive the message being sent across the synapse. You may get a better understanding of how this works by reading Appendix 5, "What You Need to Know about Your Brain."

dopamine transporter (DAT): These transporters move dopamine out of the synapse between neurons back up into the home neuron. When the DAT allows adequate amounts of dopamine to stay in the synapse long enough for messages to cross, we say a student is paying attention. See Appendix 5.

executive function: The brain's ability to organize itself, problem solve and plan for the future. In other words, a student must 1) have a good memory, 2) figure out what the problem is, 3) develop a logical plan to solve the problem and then 4) make himself or herself get started on and finish the plan. A student must have strong executive function skills to be successful in school. See Appendix 8 for more information.

fine-motor coordination: Skills required to have good handwriting and manipulate small objects.

gene: A basic molecule that determines what characteristics you inherit from your parents.

generic medication: A broad general name given to a group of medicines, for example methylphenidates and amphetamines are generic names for stimulant medications.

IDEA: Stands for Individuals with Disabilities Education Act. A federal education law that mandates that each student with a disability is entitled to a free, appropriate public education (FAPE). This law governs all public schools and some private schools. It does not apply in college, but Section 504 does.

IEP: Stands for Individualized Education Program. It's an educational plan that is required by IDEA. All students with disabilities who qualify under IDEA must have an IEP that includes a written list of learning problems and specific intervention strategies. The IEP often contains a list of accommodations that teachers must provide.

intermediate-acting medications: ADD/ADHD stimulant medications that last from four to eight hours.

long-acting medicines: ADD/ADHD stimulant medications that last from eight to twelve hours. They may also be called extended or sustained-release.

long-term memory: The place where information is stored in your brain.

Metadate: A brand name extended-release stimulant medication that helps students pay attention. As in Ritalin, methylphenidate is the main ingredient. It usually lasts roughly eight hours.

methylphenidate: A chemical used in Ritalin, Concerta and Metadate that helps students pay attention.

MTA Study: Stands for Multimodal Treatment Study. This landmark study on ADHD was conducted by the National Institute of Mental Health (NIMH) in 1997. Nearly 600 seven-to ten-year-olds were studied in the MTA Study. The most effective treatment was a combination of medication and behavioral interventions. Although medication alone was extremely effective, most parents preferred the combined strategies. See www.archpsyc.ama-assn.org, "Past Issues," 12/99; *Teaching Teens with ADD and ADHD*; and *Teenagers with ADD and ADHD*, 2nd edition, for more information.

multimodal treatment: The comprehensive approach to treatment that is recommended by experts. It includes much more than just medication and counseling. See the discussion on "Getting Treatment Right" in Chapter 3, Coping with ADD and ADHD.

neuron: The basic unit of the nervous system. The brain is composed of millions of neurons that carry messages to help students pay attention and complete schoolwork.

neurotransmitters: The chemical messengers of the brain.

NIMH: Stands for National Institute of Mental Health.

norepinephrine: One of the neurotransmitters in the brain that helps focus attention and controls impulsivity and aggression.

Other Health Impaired (OHI): a special education category. Many children with an attention deficit who are struggling academically are eligible for services under this category.

Paxil: An antidepressant that is sometimes used to treat some of the symptoms that may accompany attention deficits. Paxil is in a class of antidepressants known as SSRIs, Selective Serotonin Reuptake Inhibitors. This medicine targets serotonin and helps it work better.

Prozac: A brand name antidepressant that is sometimes used to treat some of the symptoms that accompany attention deficits. Prozac is in a class of antidepressants known as SSRIs or Selective Serotonin Reuptake Inhibitors. This medicine targets serotonin and helps it work better.

rebound effect: When the stimulant medicine wears off in the late afternoon, teens may be more irritable and their ADD or ADHD symptoms may be worse. This experience is known as rebound.

recall: Retrieving information that is stored in long-term memory.

Ritalin: A brand name stimulant medication that helps students pay attention. Methylphenidate is one of the main ingredients. This medication gets good results for up to three hours or so.

Ritalin SR: This form of Ritalin is called a sustained-release, which means it is released in the body over a period of time so it lasts four or five hours. Some doctors get the best results by having a student take both a short-acting and sustained-release Ritalin at the same time. For a variety of reasons, medications like Adderall and Concerta are used more often than Ritalin SR.

Ritalin LA: This form of Ritalin is a long-acting stimulant medication that lasts up to ten hours.

Schedule II medication: Medications like Ritalin, Dexedrine, Adderall and Concerta are called *Schedule II controlled substances.* Since the government worries that some people may abuse these medications, federal authorities monitor and control these medications very carefully. Your doctor must write a new prescription for you each month and can't call it in to the pharmacy.

Section 504: A Civil Rights law known as *Section 504 of the Rehabilitation Act of 1973,* that mandates that students with disabilities must receive reasonable accommodations. Students who have an attention deficit that interferes with their ability to learn at school may be eligible for additional support from teachers. Unlike IDEA, this law applies to elementary and secondary schools plus colleges. All school systems and colleges that accept Federal dollars must have a Section 504 coordinator.

Section 504 Plan: A plan similar to an IEP that identifies specific services that are required for eligible students.

serotonin: A neurotransmitter in the brain that helps control moods. When there is adequate serotonin in the brain, people feel better and are more likely to think that life is good. Serotonin is also very important for good sleep.

short-acting medicines: ADD/ADHD stimulant medications that last three to four hours.

short-term memory: Brief memory of about seven numbers that usually lasts up to twenty seconds. You use short-term memory when you remember a telephone number.

sleep disturbances: Over half of all students with attention deficits have significant problems falling asleep or waking up. Consequently, many families have major battles every morning just trying to get the teenager up and ready for school on time. For occasional sleep problems, doctors may suggest taking Benadryl or melatonin. Of course, don't do this without talking it over with your doctor. Doctors also may prescribe one of several medicines to help with major sleep problems. Clonidine, Trazadone, and Zyprexa are commonly prescribed. Seroquel and Tofranil are used less often.

slow processing speed: Students who have this problem process words and information more slowly than their friends. Even really smart teenagers can have this problem. As a result, they read books and write assignments more slowly than their classmates. Many students with ADD or ADHD have slow processing speed, for example, when they're reading an assignment, reviewing the questions, searching for answers in their long-term memory, and then writing the answers. That means it takes them much longer than their classmates to read and complete class and homework assignments.

SSRIs: A group of antidepressants that affect the neurotransmitter serotonin. They are called SSRIs—Selective Serotonin Reuptake Inhibitors.

Strattera: A new medicine for treating ADD and ADHD that is not a stimulant medication. It helps students pay attention and lasts all day, not just a few hours. Instead of the neurotransmitter dopamine, it targets norepinephrine. Since it's not a Schedule II medication, the doctor can call a prescription in to the pharmacy.

stimulant medication: Medications that primarily target dopamine and help students pay attention. They stimulate the central nervous system so that the neurotransmitters work better and blood flow increases in the proper area of the brain. Stimulant medications help students pay attention, complete more schoolwork, control their behavior, follow the rules, do what their parents ask them to do, and get along better with their friends.

synapse: The synapse or synaptic cleft is a space between two neurons in the brain. Messages can't cross the synapse without the help of neurotransmitters like dopamine or norepinephrine. If messages can't get across the synapse, the student can't pay attention.

Transition Plan: IDEA mandates that every IEP must contain a plan, beginning at age 14, for how the school is going to help a student make the transition from high school to the work world. The Transition Plan should include steps that begin with the process of helping the teenager select a career and learn the skills necessary for getting a job in that field or help prepare them for college. You'll find several suggestions for Transition Plans in Summary 48, *Teaching Teens with ADD and ADHD.*

working memory: A holding tank for memory where you can manipulate information. For example, you need a good working memory to remember what you want to write in an essay or to work a word problem in math. Up to half of all students with attention deficits have limited working memory. That's why writing an essay may be so hard; you have to remember so many issues like the theme of the essay, your major subtopics, supporting statements, the rules for writing the essay, the grammar rules, and then remember to get this all written down. At various times these issues will rotate in and out of your working memory. Your working memory may be too small to juggle all of them at the same time. Consequently, you may have great ideas which just seem to disappear from your brain. Reducing demands on your limited working memory capacity is critical.

Zoloft: An antidepressant that is sometimes used to treat some of the symptoms that accompany ADHD. Zoloft is in a class of antidepressants known as SSRIs or Selective Serotonin Reuptake Inhibitors. This medicine targets serotonin and helps it work better. Zoloft is prescribed more frequently than either Paxil or Prozac.

References & Resources

Barkley, Russell A. *Attention-Deficit Hyperactivity Disorder.* Second ed. New York: The
    Guilford Press, 1998.

Brooks, Robert & Goldstein, Sam. *Raising Resilient Children.* Chicago: IL: Contemporary
    Books. 2001.

Brown, Thomas E. *Attention Deficit Disorders and Comorbidities in Children, Adolescents,
    and Adults.* Washington, DC: American Psychiatric Press, 2000.

Crutsinger, Carla. *Thinking Smarter: Skills for Academic Success.* Carrolton, TX: Brainworks,
    Inc., 1992

Dendy, Chris A. Zeigler. "Five components of executive function and how they impact school
    performance." *ATTENTION! Magazine,* February 2002.

Dendy, Chris A. Zeigler. *Teaching Teens with ADD and ADHD.* Bethesda, MD. Woodbine
    House, 2000

Dendy, Chris A. Zeigler. *Teenagers with ADD.* Bethesda, MD: Woodbine House, 1995.

Deshler, Don, Ellis, Ed and Lenz, B. *Teaching Adolescents with Learning Disabilities: Strategies
    and Methods.* Denver, CO: Love Publishing, 1996.

Goldstein, Sam & Goldstein, Michael. *Managing Attention Deficit Hyperactivity Disorder in
    Children: A Guide for Practitioners.* New York: John Wiley and Sons, Inc., 1998.

Gotlieb, Ed. Personal Interview. February 2003.

Hallowell, Edward & Ratey, John. *Driven to Distraction.* New York: Pantheon, 1994.

Jensen, Peter. "Moderators and Mediators of Treatment Response for Children with AD/HD:
    The Multimodal Treatment Study (MTA) Study of Children with AD/HD. *Achieves of
    General Psychiatry.* 1999; 56: 1088-1096

Jones, Clare. "On the Road to Remember: Memory Strategies for Kids who Forget." CHADD
    Conference, 1998.

Jordan, Dixie. *Honorable Intentions: A Parent's Guide to Educational Planning for Children
    with Emotional or Behavioral Disorders.* Second ed., Pacer Center, 2000.

Katz, Mark. *On Playing a Poor Hand Well.* New York, NY: W. W. Norton & Company, 1997.

Levine, Mel. *Educational Care.* Cambridge, MA: Educators Publishing Service, 1994 and 2002.

Mayes, Susan Dickerson & Calhoun., Susan. "Prevalence and Degree of Attention and
    Learning Problems in ADHD and LD" *ADHD Reports,* V. 8, N. 2, April 2000.

Nadeau, Kathleen, Littman, Ellen, & Quinn, Patricia. *Understanding Girls with AD/HD.* Silver
    Spring, MD: Advantage Books, 1999.

Parker, Harvey. *Problem Solver Guide for Students with ADHD.* Plantation, FL: Specialty Press,
    1999.

Prince, Jeff. "Update: Pharmacotherapy of ADHD." Keynote, ADDA-SR Conference, 2003.

Pruitt, Sheryl & Dornbush, Marilyn. *Teaching the Tiger: A Handbook on ADD, Tourette
    Syndrome or Obsessive-Compulsive Disorder.* Duarte, CA: Hope Press, 1995.

Rief, Sandra. *How to Reach and Teach All Students in the Inclusive Classroom.* West Nyack,
    NY: Center for Applied Research in Education, 1996.

Robin, Arthur. *ADHD in Adolescents.* New York, NY: The Guilford Press, 1998.

Snyder, Marlene. *AD/HD & Driving: A Guide for Parents of Teens with AD/HD.* Whitefish
    Consultants. Whitefish, MT, 2001.

Thomas, Ed. *Styles and Strategies for Teaching Middle Grade Mathematics.* Woodbridge, NJ:

Thoughtful Education Press, 1999.

Welch, Ann. "Teaching Middle and High School Students with AD/HD." National CHADD Conference Program, Miami Beach, 2002.

Wilens, Tim. *Straight Talk about Psychiatric Medications for Kids*. New York, NY: The Guilford Press, 1999.

Zentall, Sydney & Goldstein, Sam. *Seven Steps to Homework Success*. Plantation, FL: Specialty Press, 1999.

Additional Resources for Teens

Amen, Antony, Johnson, Sharon & Amen, Daniel. *A Teenager's Guide to ADD*. Mindworks.

Crist, James. *ADHD--A Teenagers Guide*. Childswork/childsplay, LLC.

Dendy, Chris A. Zeigler. *Teen to Teen: The ADD Experience* (video) Cherish the Children.

Nadeau, Kathleen. *Help 4 ADD@High School*. Silver Spring, MD: Advantage Press.

Parker, Roberta. *Making the Grade: An Adolescent's Struggle with ADD*. Plantation, FL: Specialty Press.

Quinn, Patricia & Stern, Judith. *Putting on the Brakes: Young People's Guide to Understanding ADHD*. Silver Spring, MD: Advantage Press.

Index

Order Form

Please send me the following products:

Qty	Item	Price	Totals
	Books:		$
_____	A Bird's-Eye View of Life with ADD and ADHD	$19.95	
_____	Teaching Teenagers with ADD & ADHD	$18.95	$ _____
_____	Teenagers with ADD & ADHD	$18.95	$ _____
	Videos:		
_____	Father to Father: the ADD Experience	$40.00	$ _____
_____	Teen to Teen: the ADD Experience	$40.00	$ _____
_____	* Best value for both videos: Fathers & Teens	$75.00	$ _____

SUBTOTAL $ _____

SHIPPING & HANDLING: (**$5.00 minimum**)   **+10%** $ _____

TOTAL $ _____

****

Ordered by:

Name: _____

Organization: _____

Street: _____

City: _____ **State:** _____ **Zip code:** _____

Phone #: _____ **e-mail:** _____

To order:

     Mail Checks to: **Cherish the Children**
                             P.O. Box 189
                             Cedar Bluff, AL 35959

     Online: **orders@chrisdendy.com**
                             www.chrisdendy.com